THE BOOK OF
BISHOPS TAWTON

A Village Full of Memories

**SARAH AMERY, JUDY LUXFORD
AND LINDA SANDERS**

HALSGROVE

First published in Great Britain in 2014

British Library Cataloguing-in-Publication Data
A CIP record for this title is available from the British Library

ISBN 978 0 85704 239 2

HALSGROVE
Halsgrove House,
Ryelands Business Park,
Bagley Road, Wellington, Somerset TA21 9PZ
Tel: 01823 653777   Fax: 01823 216796
email: sales@halsgrove.com

Part of the Halsgrove group of companies.
Information on all Halsgrove titles is available at: www.halsgrove.com

Printed and bound in the UK by T J International

CONTENTS

Preface

In 2012, a group from the Bishops Tawton Community Ladies undertook a project to learn more about their parish. This involved the collection of memories in the form of oral histories, photographs, documents and historical news articles. A very successful exhibition of the fascinating material collected was presented in the village hall with over 600 people attending.

This book has been compiled in response to numerous requests following that exhibition. It has been written by three members of the project group as a contribution to the community for general interest and enjoyment and as a record for future generations.

This is not intended to be a referenced history of Bishops Tawton, but a collection of memories, anecdotes, family stories, photographs and documents of historical interest which are worth recording, to be accessible to all.

As the project was based on memories, some material is from first hand experience and some recalled through friends, neighbours, parents, grandparents, and even local folklore. All add to the rich tapestry but as they are memories, the same account of an event from one may not always match that of another. For the purposes of this book, all are considered of equal interest and worth sharing.

We have tried to include a good and fair representation of the material shared with us. We have aimed to enhance this with additional facts gleaned through further discussions with local people and research through the North Devon Record office and other archives. We have made every effort to check facts but no doubt will have made some mistakes and for this we apologise in advance for any misunderstanding or offence caused.

Finally, we would like to say that the collection of material throughout the project, and the subsequent production of this book have only been made possible by the willingness and co-operation of so many people who have a connection to and a love of Bishops Tawton. For this we thank you all.

We very much hope that you will enjoy reading it.

Sarah Amery, Judy Luxford, Linda Sanders.

Acknowledgements

The authors would like to thank the following people for their contributions and support, willingly given in many different ways over the length of this project:

They would also like to acknowledge the special part played by Lorna Holland who gave so much to this community and showed such enthusiasm for the project, but sadly passed away before seeing the finished book.

Patricia Andrew
Bill Babb
Andy Bament
Bob Barrow
Brian Barrow
Michael & Stella Beer
Mark & Jean Brace
Claire Campbell-Lamerton
Mary Courtenay
Sally & Ron Crook
Lynn Dare
Cyril Dennis
Ronald Down
Grace Elliott & Family
Mavis Easteau
Jean Ford
Mike Ford
Shirley & Leslie Geen
Lorie Harding
Wendy Heale
Lorna Holland
Catherine Jones
Sally Joy
Ricky Knight
Alan & Zena Knight
Janet Law
The Lewis family
Sylvia Luxton
Dianne Lyddon
Colonel & Mrs Maxse

Bob Mellows
Chris & Marion Morrison
Fred Ovey
Betty Partridge & Family
Lucy Rosser
Megan Runnalls
Robert & Anne Sherlock
Andy Shiner
Christine Shapland
John Shapland
Elvie Snow
Cynthia Snowdon
Andrew Spear
Phyllis Spear
Roy & Jean Shapland
Diane Smale
Mike & Diana Snell
Sue Squire
Kieron Stancombe
Jenny & Alf Stevens
Charles & Jane Stanbury
John Taylor
Sue Threakall
Hugh Thomas
James & Jill Waldron
Diana Verney
Joan Warren
Denise Webber
Vicki White
Pat Wright

We would also like to extend our special thanks to:

The Bishops Tawton Community Ladies for their help, particularly Pam Lewis, Jo Pay and L'Anne Knight for their input to the original memories project.

The staff of the North Devon Record Office and of the Barnstaple Athenaeum for their continued help and support.

The Beaford Archive, the *North Devon Journal*, the *Express and Echo* and Tempest Photography for permission to use archive material.

The children, teachers and governors of Bishops Tawton School for their contributions and permission to use material.

Steve Thomas for his help with additional photography

Our apologies to anyone else who has helped us in any way but who we may have inadvertently left off this list.

Lastly, enormous thanks to our long suffering husbands for their patience and support throughout this project.

Introduction

This book does not intend to be a definitive history of the parish of Bishops Tawton: it is a collection of memories and photos that people have shared with us. However it seems important to set the memories in an historical context.

Bishops Tawton is an ancient parish and featured in the Domesday Book, where it was described as constituting:

"12 hides; 3 of them have never paid tax but only 9 have. In lordship 6 ploughs: 18 slaves: 3hides.
80 villagers and 11 small holders who have 100 ploughs.
22 pigmen who pay 100 pigs; meadow 24 acres; pasture 100 acres; underwood 12 acres.
1 cob; 15 cattle; 153 sheep."

It is a small village on the east side of the River Taw 2½ miles from Barnstaple. Bishop's Tawton was reputed to be a seat of the Bishop of Exeter in the early forteenth century and Court Farm, in the centre of the village, is said to have been the site of the bishop's palace. This has been much debated but although widely believed to be true is not proven.

In 1348 there was an invasion of the manor of Bishops Tawton. A large contingent of men, including some names still familiar today, mostly from Toriton (Torrington) invaded the village.

"... a great multitude, confederate and sworn together, and furnished with arms, coming to the manor of Tauton Bishop's, co. Devon ... by night invaded the manor, broke the close, gates, doors and bars of the house of the manor, and entering the houses drove away 200 oxen, 100 cows, and 1000 sheep, worth 500 marks, and had their will of them, carried away his goods, and assaulted his men and servants." Taken from the Calendar of the Patent Rolls. Edward 111 Volume 8 (1348-1350).

A fierce battle occurred during the Civil War with opposing sides firing at each other across the Taw. A canon ball from that time became embedded in a wall of the old building at Court Farm and it remains at the house to this day.

At times Bishops Tawton has achieved notoriety. According to the Diocesan Registry there was a murder in the parish in 1383. John Rasseaghe senior and his son John were excommunicated for murdering Master Richard Wode on 20 August 1383. Richard Wode was the Chaplain of Newport at the time, and P.C. Boughton, famous for being the arresting officer of John Lee in 1885 "the man they couldn't hang" retired to the village and spent his last days here.

Happily Bishops Tawton seems a more peaceful place in present times. There are lovely walks to be had on Codden Hill, along the River Taw and the Tarka Trail passes through the village. The scenic railway route to Exeter, known as the Tarka Line, also runs through Bishops Tawton. There is no station or halt here although there have been campaigns at various times to provide one. Historically Bishops Tawton has been written in various forms – Bishopstawton, Bishop's Tawton, Bishops Tawton. The authors decided, despite the grammatical inaccuracy of omitting the apostrophe, that they would adopt the version most often used today, ie Bishops Tawton.

Despite it's proximity to Barnstaple and the changing lifestyle of the twentieth and twenty-first centuries, Bishops Tawton manages to keep its individuality and community spirit. There was standing room only at a recent meeting to discuss the local plan when over 300 people came to the village hall, some watching proceedings from outside through windows. A new group of local women, the Bishops Tawton Ladies has formed and organises social and fund raising activities. There is a thriving and "growing" allotment society and a well supported annual garden show. These things demonstrate how important it is to people living in the parish to retain the character of this special place.

Chapter 1

A Little Taster

The following photographs were collected as part of the research for this book but have not all been used in the chapters. The authors however felt these were worth sharing.

Bishops Tawton was certainly a quieter place in the past, untroubled by passing traffic. Ronald Down, who is now one hundred years old remembers playing out in the street as a youngster, untroubled by passing traffic. He also recalls, during rough weather, he would be able to hear the sound of the sea as the waves travelled towards the Taw. Now it is the flow of traffic on the nearby A39 and the A377 that can be heard, rather than the flow of the water.

Above: *Francis Taylor. In quieter days retired people would be found on village benches watching the world go by. A seat under the chestnut trees in the village Square was popular as was this seat on the main road near the Elms. The man in this picture, taken in 1971, is Francis Taylor when he was ninety-one years old. Francis lived in High Cross in East Street with his brother George. Both had worked for the Bishops Tawton Morrish family as builders. A third brother, Arthur had lost his life in WW1; his brother George had seen him dying on the battlefield.*

Below: *Outside of the Bushens in the early 1900s. The Bushens on the right was known as Bushens House at this time and was all one building. A man from the cottages on the left has found a sunny doorstep to read his paper.*

Two early scenes from the late 1800s showing Rose Cottages before houses had been built on the left. This road was known as Hill Rise and at that time was the main road through the village.

Another view of the village.

The same view in about 1910 after Osborne House had been built on the left.

Hill Rise looking up the road in about 1920. The houses known as Hillside have just been built on the right.

Bishops Tawton in the 1940s or early '50s – quiet, with just one parked car. Two girls safely play in the main road with their dolls' pram.

Traffic steadily increased from the 1950s and there have been several nasty accidents on the main road. One of the accidents in living memory involved a Wallace Arnold coach in the 1960s which crashed into Westacott Cottages. The coach was carrying day trippers to Ilfracombe. The coach was very badly damaged. Some of the injured were treated at the North Devon Infirmary.

Surveying the damage after the coach crash at Westacott Cottages.

An old picture of the cottages at the top of Easter Street, taken in the late 1800s.

The same Easter Street cottages in 2014.

Taken outside Orchard House, opposite the Easter Street cottages in 1935. In the picture are Anne Smalldon, Bertha Hill, Marjorie Tonkin and Stella, the baby who would one day marry Michael Beer and live in this very house.

Another view of Easter Street taken in the 1940s or '50s. The house on the left was known as Angortha at that time.

Historically, the whole of the road from The Elms at one end of the village, to Stage Cross at the end of Mount Pleasant was known as Easter Street. There were numbers 1, 2, 3 etc in both sections. Many years ago when the village was smaller, and everyone knew everyone else, the local postman could deliver a letter addressed to Mrs G. Brown, The Village, Bishops Tawton – and it would arrive safely. As the population grew and postal services were delivered from outside the village, this arrangement became increasingly confusing.

In the 1970s the Parish Council helped with an exercise to rename some of the roads in the village using names which had come to be used by the locals. Thus Easter Street officially became Easter on one side, and East on the other. The new section of road which had been cut through farmland in about 1930 from outside Court Farm as far as The Elms had it's own sign erected: New Road.

This photograph was taken outside of the cottage on the corner of the Square and Easter Street in about 1920. Betsy Fogwell was Les Geen's grandmother, Rose and Lilly were two of his mother's sisters and Fredrick was his grandfather. They all lived in this house. They had visitors from America on the day this photograph was taken.

A wartime wedding party taken outside Cross Farm in 1940. This is the wedding of Ernest Bament and Francis Lock. People identified are: standing in the back row Mabel Morrish, Dorothy Morrish (wife of Jack Morrish and mother of Olive) while the lady in the pointed hat is Winnifred Bament, later Mrs Ensor. Standing from far right, John Morrish, his wife Louisa Morrish (known as Lucy) and their daughter Dorothy (known as Dorrie). Sixth from the right is Dora Gollop who was a teacher at Herner school.

Old view of Bishops Tawton showing Easter Street rising on the left. Tidal flooding can be seen covering the area between the mills. The Vicarage, its gardens and stables are the other side of the water. The Bushens can just be seen behind the stable block. Town Tenement is in the foreground.

A picture taken in the late 1950s or early '60s above Fair View from the field where the bungalows would be built. Again, as a landmark, the Vicarage can be seen in the background.

Chestnut trees in the Village Square in about 1940.

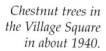

A view of Westacott Villas and Cottages taken in 1933. The Sawmills can just be seen on the right. This picture has been taken from the railway line and looks down over what was at the time an orchard behind the Bushens.

13

Shops and Businesses

Ford and Locks: the village shop where you could get anything, groceries, bacon, ham, clothes, shoes, buckets and spades and all sorts of household things.

Memories of Lorna Holland and Meg Runnalls.

Although only 2 miles from the centre of Barnstaple, Bishops Tawton, like every other village, used to be much more self sufficient. Until public and personal transport became more commonplace in the 1940s to 1960s, trips to the shops in Newport or Barnstaple were undertaken by residents mostly on foot or by bike with horsepower used by the more outlying farms. Busy village shops and visiting tradesmen were well supported by parishioners who shopped locally for their daily needs. This was supplemented by most families with home-reared-and-grown produce from gardens, orchards and allotments.

In the late 1800s and in the first half of the 1900s, a large proportion of the working population would have been employed in some way in connection with farming and agriculture, quarries, lime kilns and on the railway.

The parish was also home to a considerable number of other businesses – there are memories and evidence of builders, carpenters, undertakers, shoe repairers, saddlers, a tailor, butchers, blacksmiths, music and art teachers, electricians, a coal merchant, grinding and sawmills, agricultural engineers, and public houses. Some of these are still evident today and there is much interesting photographic evidence and fond memories of others which are long gone.

Village Shops

One of the most often remembered shops is the double fronted property almost apposite the Chichester Arms in Village Street which operated as a general village store until the early 1990s. Some of the earliest pictures of it are thought to be from the 1920s when it was run by the Wonnacott family.

More famously, and in living memory, this same shop was known for many years as Ford and Lock, run by William Thomas Ford (known as Tom Ford) and Arthur Lock. Arthur and Tom both lived locally in the village. In a 1935 directory, Ford and Lock's is listed as: Corn and Meal Merchant, Grocers, Boot and Shoe Dealers and General Stores.

Village Street showing Wonnacott's general store circa 1920s.

Another view of Wonnacott's store in the late 1920s. The man in white in the shop doorway is Mr Fred Wonnacott. His assistant at that time was Mr W. T. Ford who later with Mr Lock, took over the shop. The cart driver is Mr Chapman. VILLAGE SHOP AT BISHOPS TAWTON. BEAFORD OLD ARCHIVE IMAGES © BEAFORD ARTS.

Although a relatively small store, people can remember "Ford and Lock's" stocking just about everything that could be needed: fresh food and general groceries, household goods, clothes, gardening equipment and even buckets and spades for a trip to the seaside. There was a large delivery area covering Herner, Codden, Newton Tracey, Harracott and Hiscott. Tom Ford was well known in the area, travelling around on his bike. He would take and collect

Left: *Bill of sale from 1934 when the name of Ford and Lock had been over stamped on an old Wonnacott invoice. The items supplied, probably to the church, are a bit of a mystery.*
N. DEVON RECORD OFFICE.

Below left: *Tom Ford outside the Ford and Lock shop c.1940.* FORD AND LOCKS. BEAFORD OLD ARCHIVE IMAGES © BEAFORD ARTS

Below right: *The old Ford and Lock shop as it is today.*

A photograph taken in the 1970s or 80s during a village fête showing the shop when it was still being run under the Ford and Lock name.

Brian Ford who started out as his father's Bishops Tawton delivery boy and later developed a chain of supermarkets.

orders and is remembered by Diana Snell as never being out without his Bible. Arthur Lock would be seen driving around the area in his Austin 7.

There are many fond memories of the original Ford and Lock business in Bishops Tawton:

"I can remember a large type of cupboard to the side of the shop where mum would take me to try on a jumper or new shoes and I can remember taking in bottles, such as a vinegar bottle to be refilled from a huge pot downstairs. Where the vinegar dripped, there was a hole in the concrete underneath."
Lorna Holland. (Lorna eventually worked in the shop herself in the 1970s.)

"It wasn't self service. You would take in your list and they would serve you over the counter,. They cut and weighed your cold meats and cheese was cut from a large block." Denise Webber.

"We used to go to the village shop run by Tom Ford and Arthur Lock. Mum would take me and sit me on the chair in the shop whilst she gave over her order. This was in the 1950s. We would either carry the shopping home or it might be delivered by Tom's son Brian who had a bicycle with a little motor on the back." Janet Law.

"I can remember Mr Lock coming to our farm, on a Thursday; he would have an order book and sit at the table with Mum. Then the order was delivered on Saturday." Sylvia Luxton.

Tom Ford and Arthur Lock continued to run this shop until 1960 when Tom's son Brian took over. Brian had started out as the Bishops Tawton delivery boy for this shop but became the most famous local shopkeeper connected to Bishops Tawton. When he first took over, the shop continued with over the counter sales but in the early 1970's, Brian introduced the completely new concept of self service. Ford and Lock's, as it was still known, was the first village store to offer this. He also opened Barnstaple's first local supermarket. Brian lived in a bungalow at Chestwood whilst he began to quickly expand his self service supermarket concept way beyond Bishops Tawton. He went on to open and head up his own chain of shops and later expanded to many other areas of the South West eventually becoming the largest independent food retailer in the 1980s and 1990s.

After Ford and Lock ran the store, it carried on under a number of different owners until the late 1980s or early 1990s. It was finally forced to close for good, like so many small village stores, no longer able to attract enough local trade with improved transport and competition from larger supermarkets. Since then it has been used for a variety of other businesses including the manufacturing and sales of bespoke door knobs, accountancy and printing services.

Keeping it local: a 1934 invoice to the church for heating oil supplied by one of the village shops.
N. DEVON RECORD OFFICE.

Another well remembered shop in the village was that run by Miss L. Westcott and Miss Jessie Courtenay which was in Village Street at the bottom of Policeman's' Hill . This little shop measured only about 6 by 10 feet but in it was stocked all kinds of things, including cigarettes. The shop was known as "The Stores". This building was later the site of the last village Post Office before that finally closed in September 2008.

There were also smaller stores and sweet shops in the village. Shown opposite is an interesting photograph of Exeter Road, taken in the 1940s. In the centre, a large advertising hoarding can be seen on the side of 1 Westacott Cottages. A small shop was run from the front room of this cottage until the late 1940s.

Patricia Andrew remembers going into this shop as a child in the 1940s recalling that it was run by "Norman Facey's grandmother" who sold sweets amongst other things. Bill Babb also remembers Mrs Facey and himself as a boy taking in just a penny into her shop to buy a tumbler full of Corona, a fizzy drink widely sold locally at that time. Also notice on

Exeter Road not long after the main road had been widened and showing the shop at Westacott Cottages.

BT.25R   THE VILLAGE, BISHOPS TAWTON

the right of this picture, behind the new wall, the old coach house which had been converted in the grounds of the Vicarage. It was from this building that Bishops Tawton Post Office would be run from the 1950s until the 1970s. There are still empty fields at the back of the photograph where Mount Pleasant was later to be built in the 1960s.

Those who grew up in the village in the 1940s and 1950s can also clearly remember a small sweet shop run by a Miss Eastman from a front room of a cottage in Village Street opposite the Thorncliffe works. Children from the 1950s remember taking a step up into the cottage, into what would have been the sitting room and choosing sweets to be weighed out from a selection of big jars.

Denise Webber can remember going into this shop:
"We would go in with 3d (three old pence) and would stand for ten minutes deciding what to buy, liquorice, aniseed balls, everlasting sticks, ice lollies in the summer. She was very patient with us."

The Little Shop by the Chichester Arms

There are many memories of a small shop run from the premises next door to the Chichester Arms. This has seen a variety of businesses over the years including a shop selling knitting wool, run appropriately by a Mrs Ball, Mr Williams doing shoe repairs and as an electrical shop. It was also at one time the Post Office, run by Mr Brailey, before that was relocated down in the main road in the 1950s.

For many years though, many people can remember this shop was being run very successfully as a

newsagents in the 1960s and 70s by Bob Mellows. Bob was a local boy who had been brought up in South View, He served in the RAF in the war and later set up his own business as a newsagent. The newspaper delivery round for the parish and beyond was undertaken by Bob in his delivery van and local delivery boys from the village. There are men in the village today who recall delivering Bob's newspapers for pocket money as boys. Bob was a very well known person in Bishops Tawton, perhaps just as famous for being a newsagent as for his sporting achievements in boxing, football and badminton. Bob lived in Benbridge House in Chestwood, a house which had formerly been the Vicarage. For many years he ran the very successful village Badminton Club from the Village Hall, taking his team forward to win the league.

Bob Mellows in his delivery van.

Bob Mellows on his retirement after tenty-four years of running the village newsagents. N. DEVON JOURNAL.

The shop as it is today. It is good to see, that after many years when the shop stood empty, it re-opened in 2013 selling local crafts and produce.

Years ago, other small sales businesses would often be run out of people's homes. Denise Webber recalls Mr Skinner who was an electrician in the Chestwood area. He was the local man to visit if a family needed to collect an accumulator to power the family wireless set before electrically operated radios became available.

It was usual up until the 1960s, when more families began to have their own cars, to have frequent deliveries of fresh food to the home. The local butchers and grocers would all deliver what could not be easily carried home   Many people remember delivery vans selling fresh fish and others selling bread and other goods such as Corona.

"Two different bakers came every day, one in the morning and one in the afternoon, fish on a Friday, Lewis from Butchers Row in Barnstaple. He rang his bell, and people would go and buy their fish from the van." Jean Ford.

"I remember Mr Harper who used to deliver bread in a large basket. He would shout Baker! Baker! as he arrived." Sue Squire.

Post Offices

There are a number of premises which have been used as the Bishops Tawton Post Office over the years. A section from an old map of the village from the late 1800s shows the Post Office as being situated in a cottage at the top of East Street.

A later site for the Post Office from the early 1900s until the 1940s was the property next door to the Three Pigeons, still known today as "The Old Post Office". Michael Beer remembers his grandmother, Elizabeth Beer, being the Postmistress here up until the time she died in 1944. This is a very old building which dates from the 1600s. At one time there was a connecting door between this building and the Three Pigeons next door. It is also said that when first built, monks lived in this building.

A glass fronted extension had originally been built onto the front left hand side of the house by Elizabeth's husband William Beer, who was a carpenter, as the sales area for customers. A door to this area used to be on the side in order that Post Office customers did not have to go into the house.

The Post Office was then run for a while from the small shop next to the Chichester Arms by a Mr Brailey. In the 1950s, the post office business was moved again from Village Street to the Old Coach House on New Road opposite the Bushens.

The move to New Road, opposite the butchers, offered much more room. The building had originally been the coach house to the large Vicarage. Having been converted, the building was purchased from the Church and successfully run as a Post Office and shop for many years by Gerald and Mavis Courtenay who are well remembered in the area. Mavis had originally come to Bishops Tawton in the war as an evacuee from London, staying with the Courtenay family. She returned again as a qualified nurse and eventually married Jessie Courtenay's younger brother Gerald.   In addition to running a busy Post Office, Mavis is remembered as being a well respected, generous and community minded person. Cyril Dennis can remember when his father sadly died in the 1950s, the following Christmas Mavis very kindly sent a large box of chocolates to the family which was really touching.   Robert Sherlock recalls how Mavis ran a prayer group in the village for many years and was generally a great

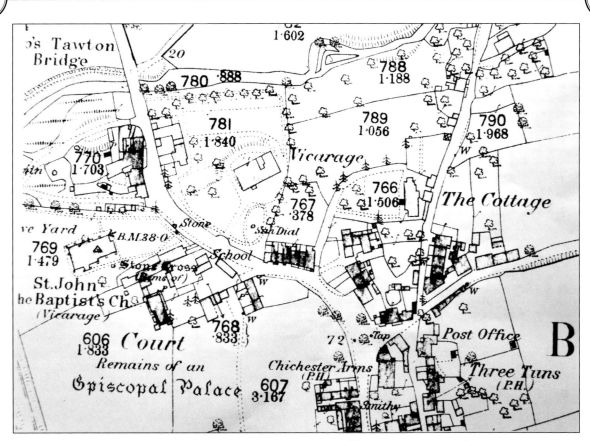

Detail from an old map from the late 1800s showing the Post Office when it was run from the house on the corner of Easter Street and Sentry Lane.

The Old Post Office next to the Three Pigeons as it is today.

source of strength and support to many people.

The Post Office at this time is remembered as being very busy. Shirley Geen remembers there were about four postmen working from this office where the mail for the area was also brought to be sorted before being delivered by bike. Gerald, as Sub Postmaster, also helped deliver some mail, covering the more outlying areas on Codden Hill and Harracott using his motorbike. As a sign of those times, Shirley, who used to occasionally cover the 12 mile mail rounds during times of holiday and sickness recalled that as was normal practice in those days she was always paid less than the men because she was a woman and that was "really annoying"! After her husband eventually retired from the Post Office, Mavis, who was also an artist, continued to run a pottery and picture gallery from the premises until the late 1980s.

From the 1960s, the final location in the village of a Post Office and small shop was the house on the lower corner of Policeman's Hill. This had also been the shop, run many years before, by Westcott & Courtenay as "The Stores". Many local people still remember Wendy Bingham running this Post Office

Mavis Courtenay.

The last village Post Office in 2007, the year before it closed.

for many years until 2001. The last Sub Postmaster was then Stephen Marsh who ran it from 2001 until it sadly finally closed as part of the national forced closure programme of Post Offices in September 2008. As with other former post offices, the property has been returned to being a residential use, known today as "The Corner House".

The Butchers

Many can still remember a Mr Isaac, whose family ran a butchery business in Barnstaple. The family had a smallholding in Bishops Tawton, keeping milking cows and also running a slaughterhouse. This was based at Rannally in Sentry Lane up until the 1940s. The slaughterhouse supplied meat to the shop run as "Benjamin Isaac and Sons, Butchers". Sanctuary Close was later built on this site. An interesting fact linked to this is that at one time Sentry Lane was known as Sanctuary Lane in recognition of the fact much of the land in this area of the village was glebe land belonging to the Church. It is quite widely assumed that the name Sanctuary became shortened over time to Sentry mainly due to the local accent.

The butcher's shop, based today at the Bushens which we fondly know as "Elliott's the Butchers" was first opened in the 1930s by Mr Reginald Slee who had come from High Bickington with his wife Sarah and eventually had a family of six children. This local butchery business was built up in the 1930s and '40s later being taken over by his son William – known as Bill Slee who had been born in the Bushens. Bill was also well known as an excellent cricketer; was on the local council; a school governor and also, in the war, a senior figure of Bishops Tawton Home Guard.

Patricia Andrew, Bill's daughter, recalls

"Originally grandfather delivered the meat with a horse and cart which was kept in the stable behind the Bushens. Later, father had a van delivering to an area as far as Atherington and Umberleigh. I can remember that on Friday nights they would be up working late till about 11pm to get all the orders ready. Father would be cutting up the meat and mother writing all the tickets."

The Bushens had originally been one building, listed as Bushens House. This was later divided by the Slee family into first two, then eventually three properties. As with most butchers of the time, slaughtering of local animals was originally done on site. Local farmers brought animals as indeed did some local people who had kept and fattened a pig. They would bring it to Mr Slee to be killed, often paying him with parts of the pig and keeping the rest for themselves. Slaughtering at the butchers continued until the 1940s when tighter controls were introduced nationally in relation to war time rationing and larger slaughterhouses were opened.

Around the back of the Bushens there was stabling for horses and a yard for penning the animals. The animals for sale were taken into the building through the large door on the end. It is believed that before it was a butchery business, the Bushens may at one time have been used for stabling coach horses, and many years before this, it is reputed that there was a blacksmith's forge on this site. In the yard behind the building, it is remembered that there were metal rings set into the walls, presumably used for tying up horses.

Dudley Elliott (Senior) went to work in the butchers for Mr Bill Slee as a sixteen-year-old butcher's boy, eventually taking over the business with his wife Grace until he sadly passed away in 2008. His wife and family continue the business. Grace recalls the time Dudley was offered the business when Mr Slee retired. Although a good butcher by this time, he was unsure about running the business. She recalls Mr Slee encouraging him saying "You'll learn it boy!" She remembers the work being hard especially in the early days when things had to be done by hand, before new mincers and slicers were purchased. There were several boys coming in on Saturdays to help do the village round and Grace herself would drive an old blue delivery van around the parish delivering orders.

Being quite low lying and very close to the tidal Venn Stream, the butchers has been prone to flooding over the years. In recent times the shop was badly flooded in 2000 and again at Christmas 2012. Despite these setbacks, everyone was pleased to see that in January 2014 Elliotts again reopened as a quality butchers, supported both by people from the village and way beyond. It also provides a very important meeting and greeting place for the community.

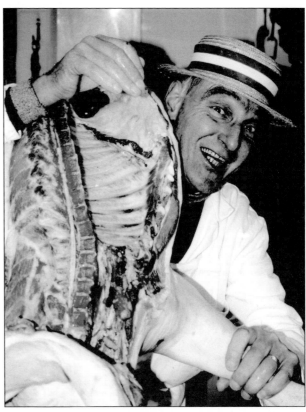

Dudley Elliott Senior. Well known and well loved figure of Bishops Tawton.

The butchers at the Bushens today. The large arched door on the curved end of the building was once the site of the original slaughterhouse – large enough for cattle to be led in.

Builders, Carpenters, Joiners and Undertakers.

There have always been local craftsmen such as builders, carpenters and other contractors based in the village. Some of the best remembered families from years ago who undertook a lot of local building work in the village were the Morrish, Pearce, Beer, Lock and Taylor families. Two of the families, as was common practice, also offered undertaking services to the parish.

Considerable general building and development work took place in Bishops Tawton in the 1920s and '30s between the two wars. This included the widening of the main road right through the village of Bishops Tawton as far as Newbridge. The road between the village and Newbridge used to have a very steep dip in the road. This was known as Milkmaids Hill; it was levelled out as part of the development. A completely new section of road was also cut from farmland, requiring the rebuilding of some sheds at Court Farm up to The Elms where it rejoined the old village street. We know this section today as New Road.

When the main road was widened and extended, the Vicarage wall was moved back slightly into the garden, reducing the size of the carriage house and some barns to widen the section near the Vicarage

opposite Court Farm. Prior to this, the road through the village that we know today as Barnstaple or Exeter Road turned up to the left at the thatched cottages opposite Court Farm to the Village Square.

The Morrish family, who were builders and at one time undertakers, had a very active local business based at the old quarry at Chestwood. There were four Morrish brothers, John, who started the business

Morrish builders outside of the Methodist chapel which they built in 1936. The trowel holder standing on the far right is Francis Taylor, his brother George Taylor is kneeling front left.

The main road through the village c.1900 before New Road was opened in the 1930s. Osborne House has been newly built on the right, but not the row of houses known as Hillside below it. This section of the road was known at this time as Hill Rise. Two old cottages can be seen at the top of the road. These were replaced by three new houses in 1910. A projecting sign advertising a tailor can be seen in the building below Osborne House.

Morrish builders working outside Taw View. John Morrish is standing at the back. The fourth man in from the left is George Taylor of East Street.

Osborne Gardens c.1940. Also built by the Morrish family.

lived at Taw View, Charlie, who was a market gardener, Harry, who built and lived at No1. Highfield Terrace and Alf Morrish, who lived at Osborne Gardens, also built by the Morrish brothers. This family were very involved in building and improvement of many other properties in Bishops Tawton, particularly in the Chestwood area and Pill Lane. John's son John – known as Jack Morrish, who lived at Rock Villa in Chestwood, later took over the business from his father.

Sue Squire, Grandaughter of Jack Morrish, recalls:
"A real treat for me would be to ride in the back of the open lorry to collect the workmen. I remember some of them: Lloyd Parker, Douglas Lock, Jack Gollop, "Dolly" Smalldon, Derek Matthews, Bert Sexon, Gerald Lynch. My Gran would get the wages ready for them every Thursday night."

Douglas Lock, a former employee of the Morrish brothers, eventually took over the business in 1968

and his family continue to operate in this same line of work today.

In the 1920s, although within the parish, Chestwood was still seen to be separate to the main village. There were very few houses in the area, just an unlit narrow road leading to the main village where Exeter Road is now, the alternative route being through Hammetts Lane. The road was widened in the late 1920s and early 1930s and many of new houses in Chestwood were built along this road by the Morrish brothers following this area being opened up.

Sally Crook-Ford says that her grandfather, Albert Ford had moved to The Bungalow at Chestwood Quarry with his family in 1910. He had been a surveyor working on the building of Newbridge. The family home had originally been designed as a temporary building but after the First World War building work was undertaken on it by the Morrish family and it remains in the family as Sally's home today. It was the first bungalow in the parish of Bishops Tawton.

Janet Law, who was born in the village, recalls that her house in Chestwood was built in 1933:
"The land here, at one time, according to our deeds, belonged to the Duke of Bedford. The houses along this row on the bank were built by the Morrish brothers who lived at the quarry. Originally I believe the houses were rented but gradually they were all sold and bought, often by the occupants. This house has always been in my family, my father (Mr Kitt) was the first to live in it."

At around the same time, at the other end of the village, further development by the Thomas family was undertaken near their business premises when the yellow Marland brick houses were built where

Alf Morrish, brother to Charlie, John, and Harry. A resident of Osborne Gardens, outside the family business at Chestwood Quarry.

The building of Highfield Terrace. In this picture, Numbers 1 and 2 are complete. To the left of the picture, Number 3 can be seen still under construction. Harry Morrish built Number 1 Highfield Terrace for himself to live in.

Tawboro: the first house to be built along the row which runs parallel to the main road in Chestwood. This was built in the 1920s for Mr Rogers. Most of the others being built later in the 1950s after the Second World War.

Below: *The same view as it looks today.*

the new road was cut through.

W. Pearce, was another general contractor and builder who lived in the parish with his family in Easter Street and undertook numerous repair and maintenance works in the village. The Pearce name is still associated with a firm of builders in the Barnstaple area. At that time, The roads we know today as Easter and East were both known as Easter. As property numbering began at No. 1 in both sections, this caused much confusion. It was eventually decided to change the name of the top section, as far as The Elms to East Street.

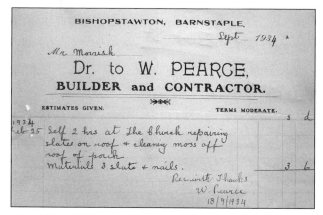

An old Pearce invoice for works to Bishops Tawton church in 1934. N. DEVON RECORD OFFICE.

Three members of the Beer family outside of their workshop in Easter Street in the late 1930s or early 1940s. From left: Michael Beer's uncle; Ernest Beer; his father John Beer and grandfather William Beer.

The Beer family have a long association with the village offering carpentry, joinery, maintenance and undertaking services. They worked with the Morrish and Pearce builders on upgrading or building many of the properties in the area. Michael Beer recalls 5 generations of his family: all living and working in the Bishops Tawton parish: his great, great grandfather, James, his great grandfather John, his grandfather William and his father William John. Originally the family were carpenters, joiners and wheelwrights, later also becoming undertakers. Undertaking was historically a locally offered service. It was normal practice to call on a local person to come and lay out the dead, and then a local undertaker to attend the house to measure for the coffin. Michael can recall the days before coffins were bought ready made when he and his family would make them to order in the family workshop. The deceased would normally stay in their own home until the funeral service just a few days later, which would also be overseen by the Beer or Morrish family firms in Bishops Tawton.

The Beer family did a lot of work at The Elms and at Hall when it was rebuilt in the 1800s after a disastrous fire. Michael also remembers that in the past,

his family, as carpenters, would make and repair wooden cartwheels which were then taken to the Thomas family at the Thorncliffe works to have the metal bands put on them.

In his later working years Michael Beer continued to offer carpentry, maintenance, undertaking and decorating services from the family premises in Easter Street before finally retiring in the late 1990s.

Other considerable building activity in the village took place in the 1960s and '70s including the whole Mount Pleasant area, Easter Street, Sanders Lane, Sentry Lane and then later again Sanctuary Close and Deerwood View but all these developments were mostly undertaken by larger developers from outside the village. Other than that, Bishops Tawton has seen rebuilding and limited infill development. In 2013 local housing development discussions became ignited again when Government-led local plans required parishes to examine all available building opportunities to meet future housing need. Bishops Tawton, with its close proximity to Barnstaple, will probably always be an area where housing development is likely. Even more need then to capture those memories and images of days gone by.

Boot and Shoe Repairers

Leather boots and shoes were made to last a long time. There are records of boot and shoe repairers in the village, three of these are within living memory.

By the telephone box in Chestwood, there is a small wooden building that used to be the site of a shoe repairer's workshop. It was run by Mr Jimmy Rogers. Janet Law can remember as a young child going in there in the 1940s and her mother taking shoes in for repair.

Mr Charlie Pugsley was another local boot and shoe repair man who also looked after all the farmers' general needs for leatherwork – a saddler. He was originally based in Holmleigh the premises next to the Old Post Office and two doors up from the shop in Village Street. This used to be a leather workers on the ground floor and above this shop, in the upper room at one time there was a "Meeting House or Room" used by the local Plymouth Brethren before what is now known the Gospel Hall was built in the 1920s. Mr Pugsley relocated in the 1930s when this building was turned into a cottage. He moved the business to a site in New Road opposite the farm buildings and carried on his shoe repair and saddlers work until he retired. A house stands on the site today.

And at one time a man called either Tom or Johnny Williams ran a repair business from the little shop by the Chichester Arms. Bill Babb can remember him fixing anything made of leather.

Thomas Agricultural Engineering Works

There had been a forge in Village Street run by the Thomas family since the mid 1800s. This is known as the Thorncliffe Works. George Thomas, a farmer's son, had come to Bishops Tawton from Rock Farm at Filleigh, a place which eventually became the Stags Head Inn.

Some of the items made at the forge were ploughs, metal wheels, gate fixings and metal bindings for wooden cart wheels and barrels. The wooden wheels were also made there using a saw bench which had been designed and made by George himself. The business would also put on metal wheel rims for other wooden cartwheels made or repaired elsewhere. Another busy aspect of the business was the frequent and regular work of shoeing horses.

In the 1850s with the expansion of farming, the Thomas family, led by George who was rather an inventor, further developed the plough which was being made by the family to incorporate an ingenious seed drill. The famous Thomas Corn Drill was thus invented, patented and made in Bishops Tawton. Originally this was horse drawn and later converted for use with a tractor. Some of the components used

The old Thorncliffe Works and the Reading Room in Village Street. Between the two buildings, a large metal ring can still be found embedded in the ground. This was the wheelwright's site used to hold the wooden wheels in place when hot metal rings were added.

An older version of the famous Thomas Corn Drill with metal wheels made in Bishops Tawton.

A newer, lightweight model of seed drill designed for use with small tractors. This drill is attached to a Ferguson TE20 tractor "The Little Grey Fergie" widely used on local farms in the late 1940s, '50's and '60s.

The unique component invented by George Thomas for the corn drill.

in the drill were made locally in other foundries, supporting other local businesses. The seed drill would eventually be used extensively in the UK and exported all over the world. In the war years many drills were made to help the war effort. The seed drill was exhibited for many years at the Devon County, Royal Cornwall and Bath and West shows and continued to be made in the Bishops Tawton works until the 1970s. The system originally invented by George would later still be found in more modern, foreign drills using modern plastic components.

The Thorncliffe Works can still be seen in Village Street. Hugh Thomas, who is the great grandson of George, the inventor of the corn drill, can remember as a boy helping out at the family works when wheelwrighting was still undertaken. When red hot expanded metal wheel rims were placed around the wooden cart wheels, Hugh had to help by dousing any burning wood using buckets of water. He recalls that great grandfather George in later years was almost blind. George had "spent many years poking his fingers into things in the workshop" and as a result had had lost quite a few of them, as indeed also did his grandfather Henry!

Public Houses

Today we are familiar with the Chichester Arms, which was once known as the Ring of Bells, and the Three Pigeons in Village Street, both of which are on the old pack horse road to Exeter. A third public house listed in Bishops Tawton used to be in East Street – the Three Tuns (an old word meaning barrels), now Number 7. In addition to the three named inns, there would have been other people selling beer from their homes over the years.

In the Directory of Devonshire of 1850, the landlord of the Three Tuns is listed as being Henry Tyte

and the landlady of the Three Pigeons as being Mary Arscott. One other person, Dorothy Richards, is listed as being a beer seller. Dorothy would have had a licence to brew and sell her own beer. In many parish records of the time, in addition to seeing many more inns and taverns than are found today, other people were frequently listed as being a beer seller or of having a beer house. It was common over 200 years ago for all households to brew their own beer. Some brewers started selling the drink but a proliferation of rowdy beer houses was curtailed by the Beer House Act of 1830. To be able to sell home brewed beer then required a licence.

Licence holders paid for either a licence to sell beer on the premises – a beer house, or an "off" licence – a beer seller. Inns would also have off sales, with people bringing their own jugs and bottles for filling. Dorothy Richards was licensed, but there may of course have been other unlicensed beer sellers in the village at that time that would not have been recorded in the official directory.

Looking along East Street today. The building on the left was the Three Tuns in in the 1800s.

The Three Pigeons is the oldest pub in the village dating from the 1600s. In 1857 it was run by Charlotte Arscott, presumably the daughter or daughter in law of Mary mentioned above. In 1889, Henry Tyte, probably the same one previously listed as being in the Three Tuns, had moved to the Three Pigeons. It had at one time a connecting door to the building next door. Originally the Pigeons had two entrance doors, both on Village Street which was, until the 1920s, the main road through the village. After the new road was extended below the Three Pigeons, another entrance was made at the back to attract passing trade. One famous landlord of the

The Three Pigeons on the left in Village Street circa late 1890s or early 1900s. The extension to the Old Post Office next door had not been built on at this time. A gap can be seen between two buildings on the right. This led up to the Methodist chapel which used to be here before it was rebuilt in the main road. A house was later built on this site. Note the magnificent village flagpole.

Three Pigeons and Old Post Office in 2014.

Pigeons in later years was Peter Hooper who had been a professional footballer in the '60s and early '70s.

There have been many different landlords and landladies in more recent times. Local people remember two in particular, John Cussell from 1977 and Peter Westcott who took over in 1996. The 1980s and '90s saw considerable change to the layout of the building, with two separate bars merged into one and the incorporation of an outdoor space facing New Road. One planning stipulation at the time was that the original external bay window of the pub had to be left in place – it now forms a cosy seating area in the bar.

The current Chichester Arms was listed in 1870 as being called the Ring of Bells. The renaming, in about 1883, took place in tribute to the Chichester family of Hall whose coat of arms still graces the front of the building. Before it became a public house, this build-

ing had originally been two cottages. Older pictures clearly show two separate entrances.

The large horse chestnut trees in the Village "Square" next to the Chichester Arms have been there for many years. Large trees certainly appear on pictures from the late 1800s and are an iconic feature of the centre of the old part of the village. These trees showed signs of disease in the 1980s and were threatened with destruction. There was an outcry and they became subject to a local "Save our Trees" campaign run by the landlord of the time, Hugh Johnson, and patrons of the Chichester Arms. The trees were saved!

The 'Chich', as it is fondly known locally, was almost completely destroyed by a devastating fire in March 2005. The fire was caused when a spark from the kitchen extraction system had ignited the thatch. Many dismayed locals watched it burn. Firemen spent the night ripping off the thatch in an attempt to halt the fire but by the next morning, only about half of the building remained. The landlord, Jeremy Clark was instrumental in getting it rebuilt using both traditional materials and methods within the year.

The Chichester Arms circa 1930s or '40s showing two entrances at the front, from the time when the building had been two cottages.

A snowy scene from the 1970s.

Top left: *The fire takes hold.*

Top right: *The day after the fire.*

Left: *The rebuilt Chichester Arms as it is today.*

Water Mills

Most rural communities would have had their own water-powered mills for grinding locally grown crops, woodwork or powering some other machinery. Many years ago there were a number of mills in the parish of Bishops Tawton, some on farms and three more central to the village. The mills local to the village were all powered with water from the stream known today as the Venn which winds its way down the valley from Landkey. The stream used to be known locally as Whitemoor Stream, later as the Little River and eventually, with the expansion of the quarry, it became known as the Venn. Back at Landkey this same stream was used to power mills for grinding corn as there were busy bakeries in that parish.

As it reached Bishops Tawton parish, there were another three mills all powered by the same stream. The first was Whitemoor Mill which was a working mill up until the early 1950s. This mill was eventually knocked down and buried in the expansion of Venn Quarry. The mill used to be accessed from a lane off the Bishops Tawton to Bableigh Road past Codden Farm and Eastacombe Cottages which used to be home to quarry workers. Until its demise, it had latterly been run by the Millman family who lived there. There was also a hydraulic ram in the river at that point supplying water to Codden Farm.

Locals remember going for family walks on Sundays to the area and crossing by the mill leat to the woods. There was also a Mazzard cherry orchard in the area.

Michael Beer remembers Whitemoor Mill as being "the most picturesque place in Bishops Tawton, a lovely old mill house with wisteria growing on the walls, on the side of the mill an old water wheel, grinding corn, generating its own electricity and powering other machines   It was all completely buried when Venn Quarry extended."

Further down the stream at the properties known today as Mill Cottages, next to the humpback bridge, was another grinding mill. This is a well known spot in the village, still very popular in the summer months. This mill was powered by water fed from a mill leat which had been diverted from the stream a little higher up, then ran over Town Tenement land and down onto a water wheel at the back of the mill. It was an overshot type wheel, powered by the weight of the water falling onto the top of the wheel buckets or paddles.

The third mill was known (and still is) as the Sawmills, which is next to the bridge over the Venn on main road. This was fed directly by the pressure of the stream when required, operated by closing a sluice gate which then diverted water to the wheel. The pressure of the water in the stream drove the wooden wheel, known as an undershot type. This wheel

Whitemoor Mill which was destroyed as part of the development of Venn Quarry.

Above left: *The mill on the stream next to the humpback bridge. Taken long before the banks were built up. Now Mill Cottages.*

Above right: *Old picture showing the large water wheel at the Sawmills taken from the main road bridge. This old wooden wheel was removed in the 1950s.*

Right: *A very old picture of the village showing the flooded area between the two mills. The large building is the Vicarage.*

powered machinery, mainly for sawing wood. Later, in the 1940s and 1950s, when sawing was no longer undertaken here, Mr Frank Scott, who lived nearby in Westacott Cottages, ran a coal yard from the premises. The stream was deeper at that time, allowing coal barges to come up from Barnstaple on the tide. They could navigate right under the new road bridge, which had been rebuilt in the 1920s, to moor up and unload.

All three mills depended on water but that water power has also proved to be a problem causing flooding at times for the two lower mills. The area behind the Sawmills was known locally in the '40s and '50s as Scott's Marsh. Before the banks of the stream were altered as part of the flood defences, local people can remember the area between the two mills being deliberately flooded in hard winters to provide an ice skating area. Many local children also learned to swim in that area and went fishing for trout. It is also rumoured that in more ancient times, the water in this stretch was used for the local ducking stool for errant or nagging Bishops Tawton wives. No living memories of that of course!

Mr Scott, who as well as being the coal merchant, sold paraffin and also undertook weekly rubbish collections in the parish. At the time, before more centrally organised council-run collections, local collections were taken to local tips. In Bishops Tawton, there was a tip of old bottles at the base of Codden Hill, another tip at Chestwood opposite the old quarry and the main large landfill tip in 1950s being the field by the river out on the Exeter Road, between Bishops Tawton and Newbridge, opposite Milkmaids Hill. These tips were a great source of entertainment and treasure for local children.

Cyril Dennis recalls from his childhood in the 1950s: *"Fridays was 'Scotties day' (Mr Scott the coal merchant who lived at the Sawmills). He had the job of collecting refuse from the village on Fridays and took it to the village tip which was at Ford Gate up until the 1960s. We boys would hide in the bushes until he had left and see what had been dumped. I was always interested in mechanical things. I looked for radios, I loved taking them apart, I ended up being a radio engineer. We couldn't afford Meccano, those radios and other rubbish we found on the tip – that was our Meccano."*

Quarries

Quarrying has been in evidence in the area over the years and had provided work for many local people for generations. Most people today will be aware of the old quarries at Chestwood, and at the bottom of Codden Hill. The development of Venn Quarry however probably had the greatest impact on the landscape of the parish.

Local people can recall their fathers and grandfathers working at Venn Quarry as quarrymen, drivers and blacksmiths. Quarrying could be a dangerous occupation: Wendy Heale recalls that her father Walter who lived in Bishops Tawton at Southview, had worked at the quarry since the 1930's. It was run at that time by the English China Clay Company. Walter was a lorry man at the quarry. One day in March 1959 there was a problem with a lorry and he

Quarrymen from Landkey c.1930's working at the local quarry. MEN WORKING IN QUARRY. BEAFORD OLD ARCHIVE IMAGES © BEAFORD ARTS.

Area covered by Venn Quarry taken from Codden Hill. 2014.

went underneath it to see what the trouble was. The lorry moved, fell and crushed him. His spine was broken in so many places he was unfortunately paraplegic. Wendy recalls that he did come home for short breaks but it was difficult for the family to cope. He eventually sadly died as a result of his injuries just over a year later in June 1960.

Another sad story is recalled by Ronald Down who worked at the quarry for over thirty years from the 1950s to the 80s. He remembers one day when someone was seen up on the hill above the quarry. The workers assumed it was a farmer looking for his stock but were then shocked to see the man throw himself over the edge. Worse still, the quarrymen then realised it was someone from their own workforce.

Eastacombe Cottages, below Codden Farm were, at one time, owned by the quarry company to have quarry workers almost on site. Most of the other workers would have walked or cycled every day from Bishops Tawton, Landkey and Barnstaple. Those who lived in the area when the quarry was active can clearly remember the daily blasting of the rock which would take place at 1 o'clock. Lorna Holland recalled how the siren was heard before the blasting which would make it "feel like the houses shook."

Venn Quarry had been one of the larger quarries in North Devon, along with quarries at Brayford supplying stone in the war years for the building of Chivenor, Roborough and Winkleigh airfields and much of the stone needed for the road development locally. It gradually reduced production, finally closing in 2006. Various alternative leisure and tourist uses have been suggested over the years for the site including the idea of sunken gardens, holiday homes and even a chairlift but it remains to be seen what if anything will happen. There has been some re-landscaping of the area in recent years but the size of the quarry can still be clearly seen from Codden Hill, extending from Whitemoor Hill towards Landkey, a reminder of the scale of this industry and the importance of it as a local employer in the past.

Apart from the large numbers of farmers, agricultural workers, quarrymen and railway workers living in the parish, other jobs listed over 100 years showing the changing range of business occupations

1850: Shoemaker: Mr Ashplant; Blacksmith: Mr Quick; Cornmiller: Mary Ford; Tailor: Mr Brearley.

1857: Chronometer Maker: Mr Whiffin.

1870: Silversmith: Mr Mallett; Stonemason: Mr Pidler.

1902: Tailor and Draper: Mr Edgar; Thatcher: Mr Rodd.

1910: Post Office: William Beer; Miller and Corn Dealer: Mr Dyer.

1919: Smallholder: Mr Shapland; Artist: Mr Fox; Carter: Mr Chapman.

1926: Shopkeeper: Mr Nutt; Boot Repairer: Mr Rogers; Egg Dealer: Mr Smoldon.

1930: Butchers: Mr Isaac, Mr Slee; Builder: Mr Pickard; Tea Gardens, Howard.

1939: Shoe Repairer: Mr Pugsley; District Nurse: Miss Cameron.

1941: Electrical Engineers: Mr Skinner; Rate Collector: Mr Beer; Police Constable: Mr Chapple; Headmistress, County School: Mrs Beer; Boot Repairer: Mr Pugsley; Haulier Mr Scott.

By 1951, the only occupations listed as active in the parish were farmers, implement makers, landlords, smallholders, shopkeepers, builders and butchers.

Chapter 3

Farms and Farming

"After school entertainment has changed a lot...I hear my grandchildren arranging to hire a video or video game to watch or play. In our day the Smith brothers would invite us up to Wellesley when their bull was going to serve somebody's cow."
John Shapland writing in 2002 in Queensland, Australia

Farming has always played an important part in Bishops Tawton life. During the latter part of the nineteenth and into the twentieth century, there were no fewer than twenty-four farms in the parish, fourteen of which were part of the Hall estate and owned by the Chichester family who farmed some of the estate themselves whilst others were managed by tenant farmers.

Frederick Dennis with Dick Copp on a Fordson tractor in 1949

Bob Barrow recalls rent day at Hall:
"When it came to quarter day the farm rents had to be paid. All the farmers were ushered into the Great Hall and given a glass of sherry. Names would then be called out and the farmer would go up to the desk with a bundle of white five pound notes and pay his rent. The solicitor would call out the names ... Anyone who had let their farms run down or had committed some misdemeanour had it brought to everyone's notice."

Alfie Stevens remembers the tenants and where they farmed in the 1950s:
> George Bidder was farming at Yeotown,
> Alfie Stevens father was at Little Fisherton.
> W. J. Jackman farmed Beara and Great Fisherton, passing the latter onto Bill Mcleod known as 'Tubby' in 1952.
> Fred Hookway was farming Westacott until 1961 when John Pincombe took on the tenancy.
> Bill Huxtable was farming Heaton and Gerald Stanbury who farmed at Halmpstone took this over when Bill retired.
> Stan Thomas farmed Lower Woolstone until about 1970 when Mr Chichester gave up Upcott and took it on himself.
> Alan Heard farmed at Shilstone, later to be taken over by David Waldron and subsequently by his son Andrew.
> George Huxtable was farming Emmett, followed by Fred Spear and then George Warne.
> Ern Smith senior was farming at Wellesley with his sons Ern and John, followed by John's son Tony.
> Tom Thorne was at Hill Farm, later taken on by his son John.
> Hawkridge was farmed by John Hoskins.

Many of these farm tenancies passed down through generations of the same family, some over several hundred years, and this continues in some cases through to the present day.

An earlier farmhouse, Broodmoor, had been destroyed by fire in May 1930. The *North Devon Journal Herald* described the event:
"The outbreak of fire was observed by W. J. Jackman, a neighbouring farmer, who saw smoke coming from what he first thought was an outhouse so he took little notice of it. He then saw that the

farm was alight and ran to the scene. He found Mr William Odam, the owner, who told him that in the burning building was a box containing the deeds of the farm and £150.00 in £1 notes. Albert John Verney who farms nearby was also early on the scene but little could be done. Barnstaple Rural Fire Brigade was in attendance under Captain Parker, but could do practically nothing because of the poor supply of water."

The house and all the family's possessions were lost.

Mr Jackman of Beara with Charles Chichester and John Shapland on the steps at Hall in the 1930s.

John Shapland, a trapper on the Hall estate with his gin traps.

John Shapland lived at Little Fisherton with his wife Susan. He was a trapper on the Hall estate in the 1930s and would catch up to a gross (144) of rabbits a week which he took in a "maun", a kind of basket, to Chapleton Station. From here they were taken by train up to London and sold on at Smithfield Market. John would leave the "mauns" for collection and bring back the empties for the following week's catch. His grandson, Bob Barrow, remembers a tale told by his grandparents.

"A pheasant was accidentally caught in one of the traps so John brought it home for supper. Charles Chichester arrived at the cottage on his horse. Susan realising that he was going to come in to talk to John threw the dinner on the fire so that they wouldn't be accused of poaching."

Farming involved large sections of the village community as well as the families directly working on the farms.

On 25 June 1915 the Bishops Tawton School Log book records that:

"the school was closed today for an extra week's holiday in order to enable the older children to help in the hay fields."

By the middle of the twentieth century Bishops Tawton was primarily a dairy farming area. In the 1950s all but three farms on the Hall estate were milking cows. Just Upcott, Emmett and Wellesley kept sheep and beef cattle.

Bob Barrow remembers that his uncle, who farmed at Lower Woolstone, used to milk cows.

"There were about 15 to 20 and consisted of Ayreshire, Shorthorn, Angus, Devon, Welsh, Longhorns and in fact a complete Heinz variety … The dogs would be sent to fetch the cows in from some far off field while the shippon was being readied. Milking was done in buckets, filtered into churns and taken by horse and butt to the milk stand up the lane. "

However in earlier times all of the farms were mixed, keeping dairy cows, beef cattle, sheep and pigs and also chickens. Christmas poultry was grown on and some farms had arable fields too. All had a vegetable or market garden. Excess produce was taken to Barnstaple Pannier Market.

Wilfred Cook who was born on Shilstone Farm, describes the trap that took them to market in his book *Count Your Blessings* He remembers a brightly coloured leather rug that covered the legs and laps of the three facing forward, children sat at the back facing backwards and the trap lamps were fitted with candles, white glass to the front and red glass to the rear.

On most farms the dairy was next to the kitchen and was used every day. The tools found there were a separator, a churn and a butter maker. Bert Verney of Overton Farm records in his book *Refections – A Trilogy of Memories* how four gallons of milk was processed in the separator each day. The cream was used for meals and making butter and the skimmed milk was warmed to blood temperature and fed to the calves and pigs. He describes how this work was done:

" At first it was done by turning the handle about ten minutes each time, but much later, a small

Excess produce was taken to Barnstaple Pannier Market. Nora Oram, Jenny Stevens' first mother-in-law, is the lady in the left foreground with the white hat.

Ethel Shapland and the girls from Bishops Tawton at a cream and butter making competition in the Pannier Market. Ethel is fourth from the right in a white hat.

petrol engine was installed. The exhaust was piped through a hole in the wall to the outside. Not very hygienic but very effective. No one was poisoned and no one had any tummy troubles."

Dairy Schools were run by Devon County Council and organisers and teachers travelled around the county setting up classes in local villages. In this photo the students are sitting at the entrance

A Devon Dairy School in the early 1900s. In the back row, fourth from the right is Nora Oram of Whitemoor. On the extreme right-hand side the lady is possibly Mrs Richard Taylor and second row, third from left is the school master, Mr Richard Taylor.

to the Old Vicarage. Children were released from school to attend the classes.

The Verneys continued to farm at Overton but after the death of Bert's son John at thirty-five there was no one to take over. The stock, cottages, off land and farm buildings were sold in September 1990. The farmhouse and cottages are now private houses, and a holiday let.

Until 1975 farmers put their churns out on the roadside for the milk lorry to collect. Most of the milk from Court Farm was taken to the dairy in Newport which was run by Nellie Waldron, sister of Edward Waldron at Court Farm.

> *"We used to have a platform for the churns and the lorry would come. And in fact some of our neighbours here, up at Overton and Whitemoor used to bring their milk down as well … If we needed extra milk we would buy their milk."*
>
> James Waldron.

The Dairy at Newport.

Court Farm is one of the oldest buildings in the village. It has a long and fascinating history. In the early thirteenth century Bishops Tawton was reputed to be a See of the Bishop of Exeter and Bishop Stapleton, the then Bishop, had a private residence in the village. This is thought to have been on the site of Court Farm and parts of the old palace remain, possibly being incorporated into the present buildings. Much research has been done and the evidence for the Bishop's See being in the village has proved inconclusive but he may still have maintained a residence there.

During the Civil War fighting was fierce in the area and canon balls were fired across the River Taw. Five lodged in the wall of Court Farm and were discovered during renovation work. Four were returned to the Wrey estate but one remains at the farm to this day.

At one time the farm belonged to the Wrey estate, owned by the Bourchier family of Tawstock Court. (Later this became St Michael's School, Tawstock) The farm was sold in the 1920s along with several farms along the Taw valley. James Waldron's grandfather bought the farm from the estate.

James remembers his grandfather, Edward Waldron, keeping beef cattle at Court Farm. They would be sold at the Barnstaple Livestock Show, which was a major event held annually in the autumn in the Pannier Market.

There was also an open air cattle market in Tuly Street with an abattoir adjacent to it, where the library is now.

Court Farm from the front.

The back of Court Farm showing some of the older parts of the building.

Local farmers showing their prize cattle at the Barnstaple Fatstock Show in the 1930s.

The overgrown approach to the listed loo.

One rather unique feature on a farm in the parish is a Grade II listed three seater toilet! Tucked away and rather overgrown now, the three holes can still clearly be seen.

One for father, one for mother and one for the children?

People were generally quite self sufficient and even farm labourers and cottagers grew their own vegetables, kept chickens and had a pig which was fattened during the year and killed for winter meat. Jenny Stevens remembers the dreadful sound of the pigs squealing when they were killed at Town Tenement Farm.

Bert Verney describes Overton as it was farmed in the 1920s and 30s by his father. It included a herd of Devon Reds and a flock of Closewool ewes. About twenty-five to thirty acres of corn was grown. One field of wheat was sold for cash, the grain sent to be milled and the reed used for thatching. Roots were

grown to feed the cattle and a couple of sows and a few hens of various breeds were kept to make use of kitchen waste.

Farmers took their animals to the local butcher, William Slee, to be slaughtered. Some of the cottagers, who kept and fattened a pig each year, also took them to him, keeping some of the pig for themselves and paying for the killing with other parts of the animal.

Farms varied in size considerably from small holdings and market gardens, like Little Fisherton, to larger farms such as Whitemoor Farm.

Robert Sanders, after whom Sanders Lane is named, owned Whitemoor Farm in the latter part of the nineteenth century. He was well known in the local community and married a girl from a prosperous South Molton family.

He kept a "Book of Remedies" from 1862 to 1874 in which he noted homemade cures for various animal, and some human, ailments as well as recording household tips.

Transcript of extract shown on page 39:

For a Kicking Horse:

Give about an hour before offering for sale:

½ pint raw linseed oil.

¼ d (drachm) of laudanum.

Lasts for two or three days but kicks worse after.

Robert Sanders died without a son to inherit the farm and it passed to his nephew, Philip Oram.

Robert Sanders took pride in developing the orchards at Whitemoor and grafted his own apple varieties. He created the "Whitemoor Orange" and the "Sanders Seedling".

Little Fisherton.

Sale of Little Fisherton, a cutting from the
North Devon Journal.

FISHERTON FARM, BISHOPSTAWTON.
Charles J. Webber, L.N.A.A., conducted an extremely successful and well-attended sale of farming stock, etc., at Little Fisherton, Bishopstawton, for Mrs. Shapland, when the auctioneer was complimented at the close. Prices ruled as follows: — Cows in calf from £12 15s. to £14 10s., barreners £14 to £17, heifers £10 2s. 6d. to £14, horse £10 2s. 6d., sows in farrow £4 7s. 6d. to £7 2s. 6d., pigs at 20s. 6d. each, and couples 38s. 6d. to 46s. per couple. Moreover, the poultry, implements, and furniture also sold well.

Robert Sanders and his sister sitting on the porch at Whitemoor.

Robert Sanders and family outside Whitemoor Farm in the late nineteenth century.

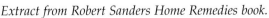

Sarah, Robert Sanders, wife, before her wedding in 1869.

Extract from Robert Sanders Home Remedies book.

Philip Oram running in the garden at Whitemoor, aged four.

Billy Joy cutting the grass at Seven Acre Field in the 1940s. He and his father worked at Whitemoor Farm.

"Some of the finest orchards in North Devon were at Whitemoor. When Mr. Sanders lived there, almost all the prizes that were won for apples came from Whitemoor. They had their own varieties."

Michael Beer.

Sadly these varieties no longer exist, though Cider making continues.

Many farms in the parish made cider. There was a cider room and press at Wellesley Farm and Bill Shapland had a press and made cider at Herner. Cider is still made at Herner, using a press that is situated in the Old School House.

There was a very old dilapidated building that housed a cider press where Ernie Smith lived in River Bend Field. Many barrels were made there by the Smiths. Michael Beer recalls that Mr Scott, the local coal merchant and haulier, would go round with his lorry to pick up fallen apples from all the orchards around the parish and take them to the shed at River Bend. There were many orchards around the village and a lot of "scrumping" went on. The village lads would also go down to River Bend and watch them make the cider, and, if they were lucky, get a glass. Jenny Stevens remembers her grandfather going to get scrumpy and some sweet cider from the shed there. She also remembers him placing a poker in the fire and then putting the red hot poker into his glass of cider to make it warm and creamy.

Jenny also recalls tales of a farm worker at Whitemoor going missing. He was later found in the cellar lying under a cider barrel with his mouth open catching the drips from the tap at the bottom of the barrel.

Jenny also remembers that farm workers were not allowed to go out and away from the farm but that when Barnstaple Fair was on, they climbed out of the window and walked to the fair.

Jean Shapland remembers that her father worked horses at Court Farm. She believes there were two heavy horses there. One he collected from Yarnscombe and rode back to Bishops Tawton. She recalls that:

"And he put me on one side and I fell off the other side because his back was so broad that my legs wouldn't go over."

Farming methods have changed and one or two horse power gave way to more.

The first tractors arrived at Horstone and Alfie Stevens remembers riding on the mudguard of a

Jo Stevens thatching a rick at Little Fisherton.

Great Fisherton and Little Fisherton in 1975.

Cutting grass for hay in 1950. Alfie and Wilf Stevens riding on the mudguard with their father in the fore-ground.

Fred Dennis driving an Allis Chalmers tractor with cousins Joe and Joyce Taylor and Aunt Bessie Adams with Wendy and Elsie in the trailer.

Fordson tractor when he was just six or seven. Health and Safety was not such an issue then!

Bob Barrow remembers the Fordson E27N that was provided by the Ministry of Agriculture to his Uncle at Lower Woolstone.

> *"... it had iron front wheels and spade lugs. We were told not to drive on the road with it but you could cross the road from field to field."*

He remembers the adaptations that had to be made to farm equipment as the shafts had to be removed from hay turners and mowers and Murch Brothers of Umberleigh were employed to fit single pole shifts with pin hitches so that the implements could be towed by the tractor.

John Shapland who, as a boy, lived at Herner before emigrating to Australia wrote in a letter in 2002 :

> *"If you have not chased rabbits running out of the corn field as the binder cuts the last quarter acre or enjoyed rook or pigeon pie then you haven't enjoyed country life."*

Sometimes the motorised version was a more dangerous option. This tractor ran away when Alfred Milton was silage making.

Threshing at Great Westacott with Jimmy Littlejohn on the tractor and Phil Hookway and his tenant.

Reed combing at Shilstone Farm using a previously steam-driven machine converted to diesel.

Modern tractors at work with the previously steam driven machine.

The end product ready to be used by the thatcher.

In the past harvesting and threshing twenty four acres would take a team of six men four days to complete. Bert Verney recalls, in his book *Reflections* that it took nine to twelve men to form a threshing team and that when the threshers came to your area you lent men to farms for a day's threshing, and when the thresher came to you, you had theirs back to help you. The teams would arrive at 6.30 am to light the boiler in the engine to get up steam and would work through until 4 o' clock or later, only stopping for lunch at around 1 o' clock. Of course all the usual chores, milking, feeding, bedding down and mucking out still had to be done, before and after the threshing.

In the 1920s and '30s farm workers generally worked very long hours. They would work from 7am

Snow and ice blocked roads preventing the milk tanker from getting through. Farmers made hazardous trips with tractors and trailers to bring milk to selected pick up points and this was the scene at Court Farm in 1975. THE NORTH DEVON JOURNAL.

Alfie Stevens with sheep at Little Fisherton. Starting young!

to 5.30 pm with a twenty minute break for "lunch" (10am to 10.20 am) an hour for a midday meal, five days a week. Then they would work from 7am until 1pm on Saturdays and a further two to three hours on Sundays checking the stock. They had no holidays, just Christmas Day, Boxing Day and Good Friday, which was often spent planting garden vegetables!

The weather was sometimes a challenge as some of the more remote farms could become cut off in snowy winters.

Jean Shapland remembers that her father worked at Court Farm and that she would help him deliver the milk. People came out from their houses and the milk was measured out into their own jugs direct from the milk churn. The measure was made of aluminium with a handle and a little cup on the end. Jean's father would remind her to only give the right amount but some people would encourage Jean, as she was just a child, to "give a little bit more like."

In the 1960s the Waldrons had the dairy in Newport and Dick Copp delivered milk by horse and cart throughout Bishops Tawton. Many people still remember "Maggie " the horse who pulled the cart. Lorna Holland remembers how she and other village children used to ride round on the horse and cart with Dick and help deliver the milk. Maggie lived in the field that became the Stanley Verney Playing Field, but was then known as "Maggie's Field".

Jane Rudgeon, née Courtenay, remembers that she and her friend Simon Andrews would go to Court Farm at lunchtime and ride Maggie back to her field. One morning they woke to find Maggie in the garden at the Old Post Office, now the Coach House.

Later milk was also delivered to the village from

Joe Stevens feeding his sheep in the snow.

Dick Copp and Maggie delivering the milk in 1965. Dick was the roundsman for twenty-one years. Maggie here is thirty-three years old.

Some of the Codden Farm Friesian herd being moved along the lane.

Maggie asking for titbits.

Codden Farm. This farm was bought in 1947 for £7000, barely the price of an acre today. One of the oldest buildings in Bishops Tawton part of the original farmhouse dates back to the sixteenth. century.

Mrs Phyllis Spear remembers how during exceptionally bad weather the tractor would take crates of milk to the Square and people would walk there and collect it for themselves.

For many years Codden Farm also supplied water to the rest of the village. A spring rises up there and pipes were dug by hand along the Venn valley to a tap on the Village Square. The farm still relies on this spring for it's water today.

Codden remained a dairy farm until 1993. Andrew Spear's father built up a pedigree herd of Friesian cattle. Every year an autumn sale was held at Codden when surplus breeding animals were sold. A record price of 2100 guineas (£2205) for a prize animal was reached in the early 1980s. In 1966 a mission from Spain came to buy cattle in England to improve the breeding stock and increase milk yields back in Northern Spain. Eleven cows were sent from Codden Farm. They travelled by lorry to Weymouth and then by specially adapted boat to Bilbao.

Other farms in the village include Cross Farm, situated along Sanders Lane towards Windy Ash. Frank Lock, grandfather of the Baments who live there now, bought Cross Farm in the 1930s. This was not a large farm but kept the usual mixture of sheep, chickens and pigs. The original house is Grade II listed and one of the oldest buildings in the village. It sits on the old packhorse road from Barnstaple to Exeter and Cross Farm land consisted of fields that ran up towards Hammetts Lane. It also included land that became the school playing field and where part of Mount Pleasant is now built.

Codden Farm in the 1950s.

Codden Farm more recently.

Top left: *Jack Salisbury and Frank Edwards pitching hay.*

Top right: *Andrew Spear's father baling hay in the 1950s.*

Above: *Andrew Spear's father driving the Fordson.*

Right: *Andrew with his cousin on the tractor in 1956.*

The building that was the farmhouse for Town Tenement Farm still exists, now two properties. It sits above the mill cottages overlooking the Venn Stream bridge. Town Tenement at one time belonged to Robert Sanders of Whitemoor Farm.

Hall and the Estate

"I remember going to dances at Hall – in the hall of Hall! This would have been in the early 1950s. I think they were probably Conservative Dances. It was all evening dress and quite formal."
Patricia Andrew and Vickie White
(both née Slee).

It is believed that in the early thirteenth century Bishop Stapleton of Exeter had a private residence at what is now Court Farm and that he gave land, now the site of Great Fisherton, to his lawyer, Simon de Halle. In 1314 Simon de Halle moved his house to a site one mile up the valley, where the present Hall house now stands.

Writing in 1965 E. R. Delderfield described the earlier house at Hall as small and pretty compact. This house became known as "Hall" and has continued to be called this up to the present day. The house passed down through the Halle family and a daughter, Thomazine, married Richard Chichester who had been born around 1455 and was the grandson of Sir John Chichester. John had married the heiress of the Raleigh family of Pilton and the Chichesters then became one of the main landowning families in the area.

The original house, medieval barn and some sixteenth century outbuildings were demolished in the nineteenth century, though a fifteenth century granary remains.

The present house was built by Robert Chichester and the principal architect was Philip Charles Hardwick, son of the architect of Euston Station Arch and St Katherine's Dock in London. It is a Gothic mansion with earlier out buildings. Mrs Maxse, daughter of Charles Chichester, felt that there was possibly some rivalry between the Chichesters of Hall and the Bourchier-Wreys of Tawstock, so that when Tawstock Court was built the Chichesters had to build a new and impressive house at Hall. The front of the house was built in the Elizabethan Gothic style. Then Robert employed a local and cheaper, architect, R. D. Gould, to design and build the back of the house, the servants' wing.

In 1857 the marriage of the eldest daughter of the "worthy squire of Hall" took place in St John the Baptist church, Bishops Tawton. It was described in a newspaper article of the time as "a scene of great gaity and rejoicing."

At this time the Hall estate was entirely self supporting in meat, dairy produce and bread, even growing the wheat, threshing it and grinding it to

Hall.

flour on the estate.

The 40 acre park was well stocked with deer until the 1930s.

Robert's son, Charles was a great character, well respected by his staff and tenants, many of whom stayed at Hall for generations. He was known for his great hospitality. The man servants had their beer for breakfast and every tradesman who called during the day helped himself as a matter of course to a jug of beer.

Every Christmas up until the First World War, a bullock was killed and distributed not only to the tenants but to the poor who came from quite a distance to receive their joint of beef.

Once a year a party was held for all the Barnstaple "cabbies", numbering nearly 50. They drove out to Hall in their cabs and were lavishly entertained in the Great Hall. Few of them were in a fit state to leave before the following morning!

His grandson Charles was well respected by people within and beyond his local community. He served as Chairman of Barnstaple Rural District Council and was chairman of Barnstaple County Bench. He also served as High Sherriff of Devon for some time.

After his death in 1995 a grand sale of the collections at Hall was organised by Sotheby's of London. More than 1000 items from collections that had built up from 1461 onwards went under the hammer. The sale was expected to raise about half a million pounds but by the end of the morning, with only a third of the items having been sold, the figure of £500,000 had already been reached.

Hall is the only house still belonging to the Chichester family. Arlington Court belonged to Rosalie Chichester and was bequeathed to the National Trust on her death in 1948 The house at Youlstone, Shirwell, had also been in the ownership of the Chichester family, but is now privately owned. Descendants of the Chichester family remain at Hall and are currently endeavouring to renovate the house and restore it to its former glory. In September 2012 a licence was applied for to hold events and weddings at Hall and more recently planning permission to renovate the oldest outbuilding there, the threshing barn, was granted. Hall's long history continues and the house will evolve and develop into the twenty-first century.

Halmpstone Manor

Halmpstone, meaning Holy Boundary Stone, was originally a manor house and it is said that at one time the Lord of the Manor, the local squire lived there. It is also believed that, when the Bishop of Exeter had a residence in Bishops Tawton, clergy making the journey to Exeter would make Halmpstone their first stop to rest and pray. The

Charles Chichester in 1964 when he was chairman of Barnstaple Rural District Council.

majority of the present house dates from 1701 when it was rebuilt, although there are beams in the oldest part of the building dating back to Saxon times. It is here at the very top of the house, reached by a steep staircase hidden behind a door, that the servants had their rooms. Above the front door an archway has been filled. It is just visible beneath the wisteria in the photo opposite above. This was the original entrance for coaches and horses and the opening continued right through the building with rooms going off in both directions. In earlier times the house was considerably larger than it is now. In 1633 John Mule, the then owner, died and in his will the house was described as having some 22 bedrooms. Unfortunately fires during the 1600s damaged parts of the house.

John Mule had no son to inherit the house and farm when he died and it passed to his daughter. This situation persisted through several generations and the house continued to pass through marriage to various owners. Fulke Hawkeye and Bennet were some of the names associated with Halmpstone.

Halmpstone has always had a farm attached to it and this continues to the present day. There is a large dairy off of the kitchen where the butter and cream were made. During its time as a hotel guests were served with dairy products made on the farm and were offered fresh milk straight from the cow. Since this was unpasteurised the practice was banned in the 1980s. There was also a back kitchen leading off

Halmpstone Manor House.

The back of the house.

from the main kitchen where poultry from the farm was killed and hung.

Stone steps from the dairy lead to a cellar and, though blocked now, it can be seen that stairs used to continue down to a further cellar beneath the carriage entrance. It is said that a "bolt hole" led from this lower cellar out into the fields. Drainage work carried out in the 1960s revealed a large cavity in the fields that would support this story.

Halmpstone has its own resident ghost. Charles Stanbury, the present occupier, tells of hearing the main front door open and close on several occasions but nobody comes through. When the manor was being used as a hotel a guest was quite sure that she saw a lady standing at the foot of a four poster bed in one of the bedrooms.

A meeting of the North Devon Friesian Society with Gerald Stanbury at Halmpstone. One of this herd won Supreme Champion at the Devon County Show.

North Devon Friesian Society farm walk at Halmpstone.

Chapter 4
Codden Hill

"The attendance this week is still very bad. This afternoon I am told that some of the boys are gone to Codden Hill picking whortleberries."
From Bishops Tawton School Log Book.
8 July 1898

Codden Hill can be seen from almost every part of Bishop's Tawton and beyond. It sits to the south and east of the village providing a natural boundary between the parishes of Bishop's Tawton and Landkey and rises to a height of over 190 metres (more than 623 feet) giving superb views in all directions. It has always played a big part in village life and has at times been controversial.

Preparing the beacon in 2012.

Bert Verney looking up at Codden Hill.

Stretching way back in time, the top of Codden Hill has been a beacon point and was one of a string of beacons lit to warn of invasion and to commemorate events. Whilst threats of invasion may be detected somewhat differently now, lighting for celebration continues to the present day. Most recently a beacon fire was lit in 2012 to celebrate Queen Elizabeth the Second's Diamond Jubilee.

Woutrine A. Bone, who in the 1930s and '40s lived at Tawton House and spent time at Town Tenement Farm, wrote a pamphlet entitled "What Codden

Robert and Anne Sherlock helping with the celebrations for the Queen's Diamond Jubilee in 2012.

Saw." She describes a rite of fertility held in pagan times:

> " ... farmers met on Codden and by the light of the beacon made an effigy of the bull in straw and mud; then each farmer made and carried to his homestead a tiny image of the bull to nail on the lintel of his farmhouse door."

Over the centuries according to references in *The Place Names of Devon* the hill has had a variety of names. In 1281 it was known as Coddeton, in 1333 as Caddon and in 1345 as Caddwillhome!

Codden has a controversial past:

In **1641** the Earl of Bedford, then a local land-owner, sold the grazing and mineral rights of the hill.

Much later in **1876** the fencing of Codden was discussed and there was considerable disagreement about the landowner's right to do this to what was considered by the parishioners as common land.

On 13 January **1880** Lord Justice Tresiger sat at the hearing of a special jury case to determine the "Alleged Rights of the People of Bishop's Tawton to Codden Hill." He concluded that it was private land and that the owners had the right to fence it. The argument was taken to the House of Commons where the judgement was overturned and requests to fence were then rejected.

In **1910** Mr Huxtable from Overton Farm, one of the landowners, complained to the Inspector of Police that four men had been caught on the hill with rabbits. No prosecution followed and a reply was received stating that Codden was not private property and could not be fenced. However a certain compromise was reached since it also said that no one should carry a gun on the hill.

In **1949** the War Agricultural Committee was pressing the owners of the hill to cultivate part of it.

It was in the early summer of 1949 that the idea of ploughing parts of the hill was first mooted by three local farmers: Bert Verney of Overton Farm, Ernie Smith of Wellesley Farm and Edward Waldron of Court Farm. Two public meetings were held to investigate the matter and at first no agreement could be reached. However later it was decided that of the 200 acres that constitute Codden Hill some 85 acres would be cultivated. Ploughing started on 20 November 1949 and a wheeled tractor and single furrow deep-digger plough went into operation.

In early December of the same year the very steep southerly slopes of the hill were ploughed with a crawler tractor. This was quite a feat as these slopes rise very steeply making the work challenging and at times dangerous.

Whilst potatoes, oats, barley, kale and forage crops were successfully grown the public continued to have open access to Codden's remaining acres.

Time limits for this cultivation were set and in **1960** a letter was sent to the Charity Commissioners in London regarding the rights of the landowners to continue to plough the hill and re-stating the rights of the parishioners to have access to the land.

In **2005** under DEFRA's Countryside Steward-ship Scheme wide tracks were forged around and across Codden that open up more of the hill to walkers and riders, though at the time many people were concerned about the effect of the changes on the natural habitat and the wildlife and some were worried that this was a pre-cursor for further development of the area.

The first ploughing of Codden Hill.

A very old photo of a Victorian picnic on the side of Codden Hill.

In **2007** there was further controversy when the parish was surveyed as part of the Definitive Footpath Review and a special hearing took place in the Village Hall where footpaths, bridleways and rights of way were hotly debated. A planning inspector chaired a meeting in the Village Hall on 19 April and following this a Definitive Footpath map for the area has been produced which reflects the conclusion of the hearing. Some paths and bridleways became public rights of way while other areas continue to have permitted access.

For many years the bracken, heather and gorse that grew on Codden were controlled by annual "swaling". This involved burning of the scrub in Spring to encourage new fresh growth and was, perhaps surprisingly, carried out by the village children.

"Every March ... for the whole of March ... we would go and just burn Codden Hill. It was brilliant!"

Denise Webber.

"We'd do it all on our own. When we got to a certain age, well we thought we were so big to have a little box of matches and go up!"

Lorna Holland.

Some restriction was placed on the children in 1915.

" At the request of P.C. Tolley I warned the children against setting the furze on fire on Codden Hill after dark."

Bishops Tawton School Log Book.

In the past the village children had much more freedom and Lorna remembers how they would go up on Codden and build dens. She also remembers the china pit at the bottom of the hill. People disposed of broken plates and pots there and the children would go and pick up pieces of broken china to make patterns with them.

Sylvia Luxton remembers the school outings to Codden. The children would walk to the top of the hill and picnic there before walking back to school again.

Bill Babb remembers the severe winter of 1947. The snow was so thick that the school buses couldn't run so the children stayed home and made their own entertainment. They went along, with the grown- ups too, to the bottom of Codden Hill.

"We went to the bottom of Codden Hill with sheets of galvanised iron, tea trays anything we could find to make sledges. We went half way over the hill and came down. If you got to the bottom you were lucky."

The Caroline Thorpe Memorial

The memorial at the top of Codden Hill was erected in 1970 in memory of Caroline Thorpe, first wife of the politician Jeremy Thorpe who was leader of the Liberal Party at the time and served as MP for North Devon between 1959 and 1979. It is made of Portland stone and set in a stone compass. It was designed by the Welsh Architect Clough Williams-Ellis and was dedicated by the then Archbishop of Canterbury, Dr Michael Ramsey who flew into Chivenor on Saturday 4 December 1970 to perform a simple opening ceremony.

Living in Cobbaton, Caroline had always enjoyed riding in the area, particularly over Codden. She died in a car accident on 29 June 1970 aged thirty-two.

In 2003 residents of Bishops Tawton walking on the hill found that the memorial had been damaged. Initially they feared that it was vandalism but a police investigation revealed that it had been struck by lightning during storms. The top stone was split in half and Jeremy Thorpe was notified and later organised the memorial's repair.

Some years later, early in 2014 the monument was again found to be damaged, this time definitely by vandals, who had scrawled graffiti onto the lower parts of the column. The graffiti was later removed.

Below the memorial is a bench. This was placed here by the Verney family of Overton in memory of Stanley Verney who died during the Second World War. The village playing field was also donated by the family in memory of their son and brother. (See the Wartime chapter for more information.)

Above: *The Caroline Thorpe Memorial when new.*

Far right: *Newspaper Cutting describing the inauguration of the memorial by the Archbishop of Canterbury.* NORTH DEVON JOURNAL.

Right: *The damaged monument.*

Primate dedicating Thorpe memorial on Codden Hill

THE Archbishop of Canterbury is flying to North Devon next month.

Mr. Jeremy Thorpe announced today that Dr. Ramsey will dedicate the monument to his wife, Caroline, which crowns Codden Hill.

The 12.30 p.m. ceremony will be on Saturday, December 4, and the Archbishop will be assisted by the Bishop of Crediton.

The Archbishop, with Mrs. Ramsey, will be flown to R.A.F. Chivenor by Lord Byers that morning.

Lord Avebury, the former Orpington M.P., Mr. Eric Lubbock, is to give a short address at the ceremony.

Stone column

The Caroline Thorpe monument, a Portland stone column set in a stone compass, has been designed by the Welsh architect, Mr. Clough Williams-Ellis.

It is Mr. Thorpe's intention to bequeath the site to the National Trust.

In today's statement Mr. Thorpe said: "There will be no special invitations issued but anyone who would like to attend the ceremony is most welcome to do so.

"It is suggested that those attending arrive not later than 12.20 p.m. and it is hoped that most people will walk to the site owing to the severe lack of space for parking cars."

Public appeal

Mr. Thorpe said he wished to make it clear that the monument was his personal memorial to his wife, and was totally separate from the public memorial fund launched by the Bishop of Crediton and others to endow the Caroline Thorpe children's ward and to benefit Chittlehampton Church.

This appeal is still open and will be closed in December.

Miss Moura Lympany, a personal friend of the Thorpes, will be giving a piano recital in Barnstaple Parish Church on December 3 in support of the memorial fund.

She will be playing music by Haydn, Schumann and Chopin.

Chapter 5

Rivers and Streams of Bishops Tawton

The River Taw flowing behind the church.

"My children used to go fishing down on the river bank and sometimes come home full of mud. They used to go over the humpback bridge to the stream there. They used to tickle trout ..."

Grace Elliott.

Bishops Tawton sits on the banks of the River Taw, rising up from river level on the eastern side. It consists of 4268 acres of land lying 2½ miles south by east of Barnstaple. The river, which flows through the length of the village and can be seen from many parts of the parish, features strongly in people's memories. The Venn Stream which also played a large part in the lives of the locals, winds its way down the valley from Landkey to join the Taw. This used to be known as "Whitemoor Stream" and later as "Little River". Many locals have both good and bad recollections of the part the rivers have played in their lives.

Cyril Dennis remembers how he used to walk into Barnstaple along the river bank.

"You used to be able to walk all the way from the village. Get over the stile next to the pumping station, through the field, under Pill Bridge, the iron bridge, under that railway bridge and all the way to town. It was a lovely walk and quite a quick way to get to town."

Local children used the river as a playground, swimming and fishing there. Anne Sherlock remembers her sons when the family first moved to the Old Vicarage in the 1970s :

"... all three of them used to go down to the River Taw ... and they all used to swim in the river and swim across."

Anne also recalls that when fishing they once caught an eel and brought it back home. It was put in the sink in the back porch and proved very difficult to kill.

Lorna Holland remembers the wildlife that used to be seen in the river, otters and great varieties of fish. Talking of the Venn Stream she recalled:

55

"I've known my cousins catch salmon with their hands in there, and they used to say we're just "tickling" it, but they used to catch some by 'tickling' them."

Areas of the river had different names. Where the river bends, four to five hundred yards from the bend was Gratton's Pit. The area where the Venn Mill stream joined the river was known as Tawton Pit and further down the river, where it became shallower, was Bedford's Beach, also known as Shelleys. Cyril Dennis remembers that it was at this shallower part of the river that he learned to swim.

Jean Ford was never allowed to go near the River Taw as a member of her family had drowned there, but she was allowed to play in the Venn Stream which was also known as "Little River".

The humpback bridge over the Venn Stream.

"... by the little bridge we would wait with stones on the parapet, wait for a tide and go for trout, or salmon peel. They came up in front of the tide. We would push off the stones then take home the fish. Mother would not eat them though, she boiled them up and fed them to the chickens."

Cyril Dennis.

Cyril also recalls that Len Snow had a boat kept above the old mill (the Sawmills). There was a lot of activity going on along the "Little River". In fact the Venn Stream flowed deeply and quickly enough to support no fewer than three working mills. Timber was cut at the Sawmills; there was a flour mill near the humpback bridge at Mill Cottages and Whitemoore Mill, further upstream where the Venn Quarry was formed and lost when the quarry was expanded, also milled grain.

Stella Beer recalls being told several stories about the Venn Stream by the bridge and Mill Cottage. This is still a very popular area. The pretty bridge and stream alongside the building has been a magnet for generations of children to play in the summer months. The water here must have been very clear. Many, many years ago, with easy access before the banks were built up, local women would take their washing down to the stream in this area using the stones in the stream as washboards. The clean water of the stream was apparently also used following the killing of local home-reared pigs to wash out the intestines before making sausages. She also remembers talk of a witches ducking pond. Nagging wives who henpecked their husbands were "ducked" in a pond between the two bridges over the stream. Fortunately a practise that has long died out!

Jean Shapland, née Dennis, said that she doesn't know what it is about water that attracts children, but it always does. She and others remembered an open area, now fenced and known as Scott's Marsh, that was 4 to 5 feet deep at times and would freeze in the winter.

"That used to freeze and we used to go in there, what we called skating but it was playing about on the ice. Always froze there, lovely."

Jean Shapland née Dennis.

Jean Ford also remembers skating on the ice a few years further on when the marsh behind the mill was flooded and froze and people took their own ice skates along and a charge was made to let them in.

Lorna Holland recalls that the River Taw would sometimes freeze over and below is a cutting from the *North Devon Journal Herald* when the river was so frozen that a man was able to walk across and plant a flag.

Sue Squires also remembers that her dad picked up a large stone and threw it on the river to break the ice but it just slid across to the other side.

A wintry River Taw.

The frozen river in the 1980s.

The frozen River Taw. THE NORTH DEVON JOURNAL.

Historically it is also known that there were lime kilns on the banks of the Taw as far up as Bishops Tawton with ships sailing up on the high tide to unload limestone and coal to heat the kilns from South Wales and Bristol. The lime produced was spread on the fields to improve the soil and increase yields. It has been suggested that it was during the Napoleonic Wars that this practice began as England expected to be cut off from supply routes. The kilns were reputedly on the banks of the river near the church, close to where the Venn Stream meets the Taw. The remains of Scatford Kiln still exist on the Tawstock side of the river.

The Annual Harvest of Elvers

Many people recall the annual harvest of elvers from the River Taw. Elvers are young eels that travel with the Gulf Stream some 3000 miles from their spawning grounds in the Sargasso Sea, in the Atlantic, west of the Carribean, to reach the Bristol Channel where tidal surges sweep them upriver and into rivers and streams including the Taw. At this stage the elvers are translucent threads just three to four inches long. Once they reach the coast they migrate up rivers and streams to find fresh water. They can move over wet grass and through wet sand.

In the 1930s and beyond the locals in Bishops Tawton would watch the tide in March and April. They would gather at dusk on the banks of the little stream below the mill, on the church side of the main road, or along the road at Newbridge and wait for the high tide. They took sieves and nets and buckets and waited for the shoals of elvers.

"Uncle Albert, Uncle Doug and Jack Knapp. They used to have a big wooden sieve and they went over to Newbridge ... they used to come back with these little wiggly worms in a bucket. But then it got that you had to have a licence and you had to have special containers. Mr Chichester from Hall would give anything to get them. They used to do them in jam jars. He'd give anything for a jam jar of elvers. Mum used to beat up an egg and then just tip them over the elvers and cook them in a pan."

Lorna Holland.

The day after catching them the men and their wives would bring the elvers in large baskets lined with white cloth round to the houses of favoured friends and sell them, a jarful for about one shilling. The elvers were put in a colander lined with salt and stirred by hand to remove the slime from their bodies. Then they were washed and ready to cook.

Some people recall having them "all alive and squirming" then fried as outlined above or put in a

A catch of elvers.

pie with a savoury egg custard. Jean Ford recalls that her dad caught elvers which they ate for breakfast with scrambled eggs.

"They tasted fishy and were silver."

Maureen Body, whose grandparents lived at Newbridge House, remembers her gran making elver cakes, something like fish cakes. She remembers seeing the elvers wriggling in buckets before they were cooked and not looking very appetising at all.

Elvers were a real delicacy. Some years storms would disperse the shoals, and misty weather made them difficult to see. Sometimes it was just a poor season. In two weeks it was all over. Locals looked forward to elvers as a spring bonus like primroses. Due to the need to conserve fish stocks fishing for elvers is now licenced and very few elvers are caught or sold locally. With dealers paying 25 to 50 pounds a kilo they are now sent by air and road to Europe, in particular Germany, the Netherlands and Denmark, where they are used to re-stock rivers or are fattened up and eaten.

Fred Ovey remembers seeing a man waiting in his car at Newbridge in the 1980s. When the elvers arrived he drove straight to London and the fish were put onto Concorde to be flown to New York and eaten for breakfast the next day.

Tragedy on the Taw

Bob Shapland lived with his mother working on the farm at Little Fisherton after his father John Shapland's death. He was just twenty-nine when he was reputed to be poaching salmon along the banks of the Taw and got very wet, possibly falling in. He became ill and developed pleurisy and died on 11 January 1933. His funeral was reported in the *North Devon Journal*, as seen in the cutting below.

Flooding on the Taw

"When the River Taw was in flood it was quite a sight and sound to hear the water rushing over the river bank and into the field which became flooded very quickly. It was frightening to hear it when it was dark and not be able to see anything."

Sue Squire (née Brown)

The beauty and peaceful sight of the River Taw running through the valley takes on a different perspective when persistent heavy rain combines with high tides. Flooding of the Taw valley has always been a problem. In years gone by Barnstaple itself would be cut off when the River Taw flooded and since money could then be in short supply the town had to open its own mint to manufacture more.

Left: *Bob Shapland at Little Fisherton, son of John Shapland, gamekeeper on the Hall estate. 1930s.*

Right: *Bob Shapland's fiancée Miss Boyles, mentioned in this newspaper report was so distraught at her loss that she drowned herself in Mannings Pit in Bradiford.*

YOUNG BISHOPSTAWTON MAN'S DEATH.

The Funeral.

It was with sincere regret that the many friends of Mr. Robert John Shapland heard that he had passed away at his home at Little Fisherton, Bishopstawton, on Wednesday evening in last week. Mr. Shapland, who was 29 years of age, and unmarried, had been in failing health for some time. He was immensely popular amongst a large circle of friends. He resided at Little Fisherton with his mother, his father (Mr. John Shapland) having passed away twelve months ago.

The funeral took place on Saturday, the interment in the Parish Churchyard being preceded by a service in the Bishopstawton Parish Church. The principal mourners were Mrs. Shapland (mother), Miss Alice Shapland (sister), Mr. and Mrs. J. Hooper, Mr. R. Shapland (Tawstock), Mr. Wm. Shapland (Tawstock) and Mr. J. Shapland, Herner (uncles and aunt), Mrs. G. Shapland, Mrs. Wm. Shapland, Mrs. J. Shapland, Mrs. Barrow, Barnstaple (aunts), Messrs. W. J. Shapland, Jack and Harry Shapland, George Shapland, Miss I. Shapland and Mrs. W. Shapland (cousins), and Miss Boyles (fiancée). Mrs. G. Barrow, Sidcup (sister) was unable to be present.

Others present included Miss Gwen Boyles, Mr. H. Ridd, Mr. F. Mock, Mr. and Mrs. E. Smith, Messrs. J. Hutchings (Bydown, Swimbridge), A. Goss (Anchor Mills), C. H. Thomas, C. Dennis, J. Houle (Fisherton), S. Gubb, W. C. Smolden, H. Harris, H. Tossell, F. Hookway, T. Hartnoll, W. J. Balman (Ford Gate), C. Sillifant, W. Waldron, W. Hartnoll, J. Facey, S. Smith, E. F. Seckler, F. Taylor, F. W. Smith, W.; Jackman (Beara), J. Isaac, Mesdames Squires, Phillips, Allen, Hookway, Hines, E. Courtney, J. Bowen, Parr, Hartnoll, Mr. and Mrs. R. Warren, Miss E. Huxtable.

The bearers, all sons of neighbouring farmers, were Messrs. E. J. Houle, jun. (Fisherton), G. Huxtable (Heaton), E. Rodd (Tanners), J. Warren (Yeotown), R. Thomas (Woolstone), and J. Passmore (Hemmett).

Floral tributes were:—From Franky; Mrs. Taylor and family, Newbridge; Nancy; from Uncle Jim, Aunt Annie and George; from Uncle Bob and Aunt Annie and family; Mr. and Mrs. Ridd and Harold; Flo and Bill, Bradiford; Mr. and Mrs. Passmore.

Mr. E. J. Beer, of Bishopstawton, carried out the funeral arrangements.

The flooded valley.

Lower lying and riverside areas of Bishops Tawton have been flooded on various occasions. This happened in the 1960s the 1980s and again in 2000. It seemed that the floods were liable to happen every ten to twenty years; however the severe flooding of December 2012 and then again in early 2014 suggests the trend is for these events to become more frequent.

There has been a crossing of the River Taw in the area of New bridge from the fourteenth century and Bishop Stapleton of Exeter left 60 shillings in his will for the repair of "the new bridge near Bishops Tawton." One old bridge was demolished in 1643 during the Civil War and there are records of bridges being in existence during the eighteenth and nineteenth century. In 1803 the county was questioned about maintenance of the bridge when one of the three spans washed away. It was rebuilt between 1804 and 1808 but was again washed away by floodwater in 1809. A new bridge was built on a site about a hundred yards up river from the old one. However because this sloped down gradually to be on a level with the marsh it continued to be very prone to flooding. On many occasions people became stranded in the floods and locals would help to rescue them by horse and cart. Finally Devon County Council and Barnstaple District Council drew up a plan for a causeway over the marsh to carry the road by a gradual incline onto the bridge. The work began in 1926 and the new road was completed and opened to traffic in 1927. Whilst the new road was a big improvement it was still not a permanent solution to the flooding issue. In the Herner School Log Book it is recorded that the children from Chapleton had to walk across Newbridge, through Beara and past Great Fisherton, then on up to Herner because the marshes they generally walked through to get to school were flooded. This happened on several occasions and was a long walk for such young children. This area continues to be at risk after exceptionally heavy rain.

In January 1968, as well as the fields along the River Taw at Newbridge, the "Under Hall road" at Herner was badly flooded and the school bus became stranded. Sylvia Luxton (née Thorne) was one of the schoolchildren on board:

"We called the driver Fred and we sort of urged him to actually drive the bus and keep on going. And he did … and we were stuck in the floods."

The rescue is described in an article in the *North Devon Journal and Herald* of the time titled: "School Bus Children escape by Raft as River Sweeps in." It tells how an aircrew rescued 26 children and saved five soldiers from death, plucking them from an amphibious vehicle that was being smashed to pieces in the foaming waters of the River Taw. The helicopter had originally been sent in response to a call from Mrs John Thomas of Brightley Barton, Umberleigh who was concerned about her husband. He had gone to bring his sheep in from low-lying pasture. He found them surrounded by water and quickly became marooned himself. The helicopter lifted Mr. Thomas to safety and then spotted the school bus. The rising water had reached the floor of the bus and got into the engine when M/Sg. Gibson was lowered to investigate the situation.

"... he saw us as he was flying, as he was going past. And the biggest disappointment was that we didn't actually get winched up in the helicopter because there were wires there."

Sylvia Luxton.

It was decided that to winch all the children off would be highly dangerous so the crew flew back to base to collect a multi-seater dinghy. Sylvia, aged fifteen at the time, describes how the little ones went off first and then she followed later. The children weren't frightened and seemed unaware of the danger of the situation. The rescuers took the children to Mr Shapland at the Lodge where they were given hot tea and then some were helped to get home by three amphibious vehicles while others were collected by their parents. By the time the last person, the driver Fred Wolstenholme, had been rescued, the water had risen above the level of the bus seats.

In an interview with Patricia Andrew, she vividly recalls being flooded when newly married and living next door to her father William Slee, the butcher, at the Bushens.

"Firstly in the 1960s I can remember it was a Sunday. My husband said he would go down to the bridge and watch the water come up. It came up so quickly, by the time he came back the water had reached just under the top of the table ... all I could see was the tea on the table."

She describes the terrible mess and smell that the flood caused and also how the water had a slick of paraffin floating on top. There was a coalyard, Scotts, across the road and the floodwater tipped over the containers and spilt the paraffin. The water went away quickly but left a dreadful mess and smell. She remembers it all happening again about ten years later when her mother lost a lot of personal possessions in the flood.

Many people recall the floods of 1980s. Following these the National River Authority worked on the banks of the Venn Stream, installing very large boulders on the side of the stream opposite Valley Cottages. The work was completed in 1989 and intended to prevent flooding in the area in future. However Jo Pay recalls that Valley Cottages were again flooded in 1995 and 1996.

One of the the most severe floods in living memory occurred in October 2000 at the end of a very wet summer. It had rained continually during the previous week and Jo remembers getting up regu-

Fg. Off. McGregor, pilot, Flt. Lt. Funnell, navigator and M/Sg. Gibson, winchman. The crew that rescued the school children.

larly during the night to monitor the situation and to move things , initially to table tops and then upstairs. Early in the morning the flood waters rose and despite it being a beautiful bright morning people were evacuated from their houses.

There was no way to walk from one side of the village to the other as all roads and paths over the River and stream were flooded. A boat was commandeered from a resident of the Law Memorial Houses by the fire brigade and used to ferry people across.

Another extremely bad flood occurred in December 2012, just two days before Christmas. Trish Pay of Valley Cottages explained that the water would rise in her cottage to about 11 inches fairly often and there was a mark on the wall to indicate this. In November 2012 the water rose to about 8 ½ inches but quickly receded. In December it happened again and began to go down. Jo and Peter Pay climbed over the flood boards and walked into the village to see how others likely to flood had fared. They then realised that the water was rising again and hurried back home. This time both cottages were severely flooded with the water rising above waist level. The Sawmills and the Bushens were also

Looking from Valley Cottages towards the humpback bridge in the October floods of 2000.

Firemen ferrying people from one side of the village to the other.

A boat was also needed at Valley Cottages.

In 2000 as the flood water receded the extent of the damage in School Lane became clear.

conveyor belt of people formed. Meat was passed down the chain of fifteen or more helpers to a refrigerated van and transported to Fishleigh Barton where a recently closed butcher's shop provided the facilities needed to complete the preparation of turkeys and other meats.

Following this flood much work was done by the Parish Council, in conjunction with South West Water and the Enviroinment Agency, looking at ways to avert the risk of flooding in the future.

As well as the lack of dredging, many people feel that blocked storm drains, poor maintainance by South West Water and building development upstream are factors leading to the increased frequency of flooding events. Issues with the disused quarry and the maintenance of the lagoon there have also been raised. Others blame the changing weather patterns due to global warming. This debate continues nationally. At different times various flood defence schemes have been put in place. The banks of the Taw have been raised to contain the river when it runs high. Chris Morrison recalls moving into Mill Cottage in 1979 and being flooded three times in their first year there. Since then retaining walls have been built along parts of the Venn Stream to protect the buildings there. Some recommended measures require funding which is not presently available but other steps have been taken and plans put in place. Improved retaining walls have been built by the Venn Stream. The Parish Council has a local flood plan with a list of people willing to be called on in the event of a flooding threat. The Environment Agency sends someone to monitor what is happening where previously all decisions were taken in Exeter.

Although the Taw and the Venn Stream used to support a lot of wild life (Lorna Holland remembers

affected by flood water from the Taw and the Venn Stream seeming to surge in both directions. Thousands of pounds worth of damage was caused to homes and businesses but a community spirit prevailed as villagers rallied round to help. Families slept in the Village Hall and people brought food and sleeping gear for them.

At the Old Vicarage, opposite the hall, a line of fridges stood in the hallway. Quick action to remove well stocked fridges and freezers bulging with food bought for the Christmas holiday saved many people's Christmas lunch!

The Bushens was very badly affected and even a pet duck was drowned. Elliotts the butchers was flooded and to save Christmas meat orders a

The dredging of Venn Stream was thought to be one solution.

Working to dredge the Venn as it passes under the humpback bridge.

otters and salmon in the stream) this is less so today. Silting of the river and a general decline in these species, is probably the reason, though pollutants cannot be ruled out completely. In April 2007, following the closure of the Venn Quarry in the previous September, Marion and Chris Morrison noticed that, where the stream flowed past their cottage and on under the bridge, it was turning a strange bluey green colour. At the time a thick sediment was also coating rocks and the stream bed. The Environment Agency tested the water and revealed higher than normal levels of minerals including zinc, copper, cobalt, iron and magnesium and a greater number of dead fish than usual. Looking further into this it was found that water from the lagoon at the quarry was no longer being purified and pumped away. The water level there had risen to 3 to 4 feet above the permitted level. Steps were taken to ensure that the lagoon continued to be properly managed and maintained and the water is running clear at the present time.

Fun and Games on the River

The River Taw is not just seen as a threat to the inhabitants of Bishops Tawton. It has always provided opportunities for fun and enjoyment. As well as swimming and fishing there many people remember the raft races that took place in the 1980s.

> "It was lovely. All the village, well it seemed like all the village used to go there and wait for them to come down and then we'd all cheer and clap … usually it was a nice warm day and people took something to eat and drink down there."
>
> Grace Elliott.

The race began at Umberleigh and the rafts would race back down the river, through the area behind the Bushens known as Shelleys, all the way to Barnstaple. Here a crane was employed to pull the rafts back out of the river.

Grace recalls one year when young Dudley's raft turned over and got stuck in the mud. Apparently they wanted to give up but people helped them right the raft and they were able to carry on to the finish. Katie's raft also overturned and no one came to the rescue, but somehow they got it back up and finished the race.

On another occasion a different kind of race was organised. This time not rafts but plastic ducks made their way along the little river. They were put into the water upstream of Codden Farm, around Eastacombe cottages. Each was marked to identify the owner and they made their way downstream to the humpback bridge by Mill Cottages. Unfortunately, the course of the Venn Stream, and the race, did not run smoothly! The stream meanders and winds along the valley and most of the ducks became stuck

A raft race on the River Taw in the 1980s.

Lining up at the start.

in the mud and wedged against the bank. This race did not become a regular feature of fêtes and celebrations in the village.

Fun continues on the Taw today, when the tide is right kayakers and occasional water skiers can be seen and a Gentleman's Paddle Club has recently been formed with members paddling both on the coast and along the Taw.

Chapter 6
Churches and Chapels

"The weather was beautiful the atmosphere electric. The memories of the past building – where you felt like a bird with its nest in a crevice in the wall – and now a new home had been built with open space around, and blue sky above."

A quote from opening of the new Methodist chapel, from the 50th Anniversary brochure.

There are three places of formal worship in the village, the parish church of Saint John the Baptist, the Methodist chapel and the Gospel Hall. Herner church also stands within our parish. National ideas and the enthusiasm of individuals have influenced the history of them all and the way they have developed over the years. They are, of course, still evolving.

The Parish Church of Saint John the Baptist

Bishops Tawton is a very ancient parish. It is said by many to have the oldest church in Devon.

It is often reported that Bishops Tawton was a very early See for the Bishop of Exeter until Putta, the second Bishop, removed the See to Crediton. Although widely believed and often written, we have been told that this has been difficult to prove and the debate goes on. It is thought that the Bishop continued to have a palace in the village long after the See was removed and traces of the original palace building have been incorporated into the house at Court Farm; there are records of priests being ordained there, according to one source.

The present church dates from 1340 but there was a church on that site before that time. The north aisle

Saint John the Baptist church, Bishops Tawton.

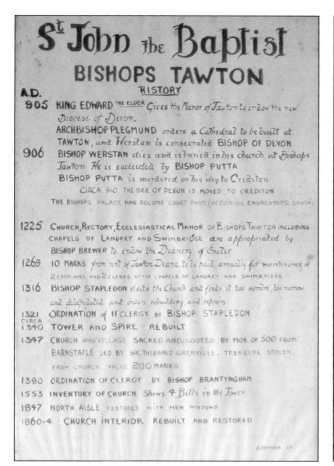

This hangs inside the church porch and gives an interesting historical account of the church.

Past vicars at St John the Baptist church. This hangs inside the church.

was added in about 1450 and the chancel was rebuilt in 1864. The flat roof of the north aisle dates from about 1877 and replaced a pitched roof. The crocketted octagonal medieval spire is a great rarity in Devon.

In the vestry there is a sanctuary ring. This used to be on an outside door. If a fugitive touched the ring he was given sanctuary in the church and avoided arrest.

Michael Beer tells us there used to be a gallery and on the outside wall you can see the shape of the door into the gallery. It was taken down in Victorian times, when they also put in new pews and a new west window. The boards in the vestry with words about charity to the poor, were part of the gallery.

Vicars of Bishops Tawton

There have been several others since the list above was completed. The more recent ones are John Carvosso, Bill Benson, John Benson, Paul Neimic, and now at the time of writing Andy Dodwell.

The Vicarage, or the Parsonage as it was sometimes called, was built in 1841 at a cost of £1680. It was a huge house with its own well, and stores in the cellar for wine, beer and coal. It was built in three storeys with accommodation for servants on the top floor. On the ground floor there was a drawing room, dining room, study, kitchen, scullery, pantry, dairy, larder, servants' hall and workroom. There were four bedrooms for the vicar's family, three of which had separate dressing rooms, a day nursery, a night nursery and a schoolroom. On the second floor there were four more bedrooms for the servants.

In 1950 the Rev. Geoffery Kestell Cornish, the vicar at the time and the Church Commissioners for England sold it to Brake & Co. Ltd. It was divided into three private houses and sold. The Coach House was sold as another separate dwelling. The Rev. Cornish recalls the house was far too big and very cold and repairs were very expensive. He also recognised the changed role of the vicar and said that vicars were no longer such important people as they used to be. After he moved and the house was sold the vicar moved to Bembridge and this became the new Vicarage. Now there is no vicarage at all in Bishops Tawton and we share a vicar with Newport.

The Vicarage.

Choir

Times have changed! The Bishops Tawton choir has matured!

There was a large choir in the past. Michael Beer remembers how he came to join the choir in around 1943. When he was a child, he was one of over 30 children in the Sunday School taught by Miss Holland. She told Parson Nicholas that it was time Michael joined the choir. He was the youngest in the choir at that time. He remembers that the choir stalls were full, with two extra rows of seats that have been removed now. There was no room for him and he had to sit on a chair on the end! Being in the choir took a lot of time; there were two services on a Sunday where they sang, as well as often a baptism in the afternoon. They had a practise in the week too. He remembers the choirmaster and organist was Stanley Brent; he played for them for over thirty years. Choirboys were paid a small amount of money to encourage attendance but for Michael this was not important, as he loved the music. At Christmas time there was a party for the choir and bell ringers but this stopped during the war.

Cyril Dennis remembers being a choirboy at the church. He remembers the Rev. Goatman in the 1950s. There was always a full Sunday School and lots of children in church. He remembers Mr Brent was the choirmaster. He tells us the choir stalls were always full and he felt that it may have been something to do with the fact that they got a shilling for being in the choir!

The choir were still paid in 1980s. They attended the Morning service, Evensong and weddings, as well as weekly Friday night practice sessions.

The choir in 1980s, Nick Guy, Linda Evans, Gary Evans and Alex Guy.

This shows the size of the choir in the past. It is the wedding of Jean Brent. Her father was the church organist for many years. Several singers were named at the Memories Exhibition, Grace Elliot, Brian Gilbert and Michael Toller.

Induction at Church in 1953. FROM NDJ ATHENAEUM COLLECTION ND RECORD OFFICE.

A wonderful account of a glamorous Bishops Tawton Wedding 25 August 1857

"This morning the village of Bishops Tawton was the scene of great gaiety and rejoicing on the occasion of the marriage of the eldest daughter of the worthy squire of Hall. At an early hour the bells of the parish steeple awoke the melody of the feathered songsters and ere long the villagers were astir. The national banner was hoisted over the clock tower, and a beautiful arcade of evergreens and flowers surmounted with four tricoloured flags erected over the principal entrance to the churchyard, having on the east end the initials of the bride, A.C. and on the west those of the bride and bridegroom. The principal inn of the village was decorated with flags and evergreens: and a neat festoon with streamers was hung in mid air by the occupier of the home farm (Mr Waldron), to testify his respect for his landlord and the family. These were the only decorations we noticed! The wedding party set out from Hall in the following order:-

First carriage (Mr Fulford's), containing Baldwin Fulford Esq of Great Fulford, Dr Holland (uncle of the bridegroom) of Lyncroft Hall and Stow and Mrs Lambert of the Vineyard, Exeter.

Second carriage, Mrs Chichester, of Hall, and Mr and Mrs William Chichester, of Grenofen.

Third carriage, five of the bridesmaids (the others joined the party at the church), Mr Charles Chichester, Mr Harris, of Portchester-square, and Mr Chatfield.

Fourth carriage, Mr and the Misses Erskine, of Ilfracombe.

Fifth carriage, Charles Henry Webber Esq., of Buckland House, and family. Sixth carriage, the bridegroom Richard Leigh Holland Esq., of Queen Anne- Street, Regents Park, and his 'bestman' Charles Leathley, Esq.

Seventh, the Hall carriage, the bride, Miss Anne Chichester, and her father, Robert Chichester, Esq.

A large company of the neighbouring gentry awaited their arrival at the church, where the ceremony was performed in the presence of a brilliant circle by the respected vicar of the parish, the Rev. John Durand Baker. The brides maids were, Miss Clara Chichester, Miss Gertrude Chichester, Miss Elizabeth Chichester, Miss Margaret Chichester (the lovely sisters of the bride). A fairer galaxy will not be seen in a day's journey. The bride was attired in a rich white silk dress, with Honiton lace flounces; her head was encircled with an elegant wreath of orange blossoms and Stephanotis, from which was pendant and superb bridal veil of Honiton lace.

This shows the funeral of P.C. Boughton. Six policemen were the bearers, Sergeant Charlie was recognised as the policeman in uniform who was standing by the pillar. It also shows the old road before widening took place.

The funeral of a member of the Chichester family.

Hall is approached from the turnpike by a carriage drive of more than a mile in length, through a double row of oaks; it is a noble Elizabethan mansion, situated on an eminence, with a southern aspect, embosomed amidst stately trees now covered with verdant foliage. A shady avenue of sycamores leads direct from the garden front and divides the deer park from the lawn. In the deer park itself is a fine herd of fallow deer, which may be seen from several windows of the house, the flower garden alone intervening. In the mansion and its belongings is displayed the highly cultivated taste of the owner, who has spared no expense to render Hall one of the most attractive country seats in the neighbourhood.

The dejeuner was laid out in the great hall, a splendid room, in the old style of architecture, 42ft long and 36 ft 9in high – the roof of solid oak. In the centre of the table, which extended the entire length of the hall, was the bride cake, a rich and beautiful specimen of the confectioner's art. It was surmounted by a temple of Hymen, was frosted over and surrounded with white monuments of almost every device; the base was adorned with a wreath of natural flowers, principally orange blossoms. The dejeuner, it is needless to observe, embraced every luxury that could tempt the most fastidious palate. The fruits were from the celebrated gardens and conservatories of Hall, the wedding cake from London. The guests numbered above forty."

From an unidentifiable source at the North Devon Record office.

Renewal of Vows

In June of 1985 the Rev. John Carvosso at St John the Baptist church gathered 200 people together to renew their marriage vows. There was a exhibition of wedding photographs over six decades. There was also a flower festival to celebrate the event.

P.C. Boughton's Funeral

P.C. Boughton worked in Babbacombe. He was the arresting officer of a murderer, John Henry George Lee, who was more commonly known as John Babbacombe Lee. In 1885 he was found guilty and sentenced to hanging. After three attempts to hang him he was given a pardon and released. After retirement P.C. Boughton lived in Bishops Tawton. He was commended for his service to the force. See photograph opposite.

Chichester Vault

Michael Beer remembers, the Chichester vault. He says that most of the Chichester family were buried in the vault underneath the church but eventually the vault was filled up. The last Mr Chichester and his wife were buried at Herner. He recalls his father, who was the undertaker, saying,

"Whenever you get a funeral of the Chichesters and they mention Herner, try to avoid it like the plague!"

He explains that his father was involved in the burials and in those days they had no machines and they had to dig in solid rock at Herner using a jack-hammer. They even had to delay the date of one funeral because the grave was not ready.

The Bishops Tawton bells 1907. Mr R. Chichester of Hall, Mr Davie, Rev. Lester, Mr Dart the blacksmith, Mr John Beer.

Bells

The bells have a history of their own.

A document tells us that before 1803 there were only four bells in the tower. In that year the four bells were recast into five by Thomas Bilbie of Cullompton The fourth and the tenor were 'miserably bad' and the second was 'indifferent besides being too light in metal'. In 1825 at the suggestion of Mr R. Chichester, the then churchwarden, the fourth and tenor were recast and a treble added. These three bells were cast in Oxford by W. J. Taylor. In 1831 more metal was added to the third, which was recast by John Taylor at Buckland Brewer. At that time the five other bells were retuned. On the third bell there is a verse inscribed,

"Should I be found to speak with grace and ease,
And, with my fellows, all my hearers please,
To great delight of me, the third, shall be,
To sound the praises of the Trinity."

There is a document from 1853 that tells of the village being denied the pleasure of hearing our "lively ring of bells, to perfection" as the third bell was cracked. The bell was recast, as well as the treble, that was out of tune. On Easter Monday, 28 March 1853 at an early hour in the morning a flag was hoisted above the tower and at 6 am the houses near the church were disturbed by a "merry Peal" which was well rung by the best set of the "Tawton youths". The Tawton Men, assisted by able ringers from Landkey rang the bells again at 10 am! In the course of the day several peals of rounds and some changes were rung in "good style". At least 20 peals were rung before 7 pm. The occasion was celebrated by a dinner at the Duke of Bedford's Courthouse provided by Robert Chichester, the vicar, and the principal rate payers, for the entertainment of the ringers. They all sat down to the dinner that consisted of two rounds of beef and a fine leg of mutton of 15lbs. Plum pudding was served up from the Three Pigeons. Some young ladies, during the retirement, of the ringers took possession of the belfry and succeeded in "making the bells speak". During the evening the principal farmers and ringers adjourned to the Three Pigeons where they cheered repeatedly with "a pie in hand and a cup of famous ale"! Some time in the afternoon a steeplejack climbed to the top of the spire and his head made contact with the weathercock on the top.

(From the opening of the bells, Printed by G.N. Jenvey, printer and book seller, High St, Barnstaple.)

In 1907 the bells were re-examined and it was discovered that the oak beams supporting the bells had become dangerously rotten. The restoration work was estimated at £200. Mr Chichester of Hall raised £130 and it was decided to sell off the old woodwork as mementos. The renovation committee went around the village to raise money. The vicar at the time, Rev. E. Lester said, "the bells are for the use of the whole of the parishioners and we look with confidence to them for support." A cast iron frame was installed and this meant that the tenor bell could be hung alongside the other bells instead of in the steeple where it had been.

An ancient looking document in the tower tells us about the size and weight of the bells at Bishops Tawton. It appears to date from the 1800s.

Treble	2 feet 4 inches	5 cwt	0 quarters	9 lbs
Bell 2	2 feet 5 inches	5 cwt	1 quarter	0 lbs
Bell 3	2 feet 7 inches	6 cwt	0 quarter	5 lbs
Bell 4	2 feet 8 inches	6 cwt	2 quarters	0 lbs
Bell 5	2 feet 10 inches	7 cwt	3 quarters	18 lbs
Tenor	3 feet 2 inches	10 cwt	1 quarter	9 lbs

Above: *This picture shows the gathering after the rehanging of the bells.*

Left: *These are the bell ringers outside the belfry door. It is thought to date from around 1900. Mr Dart, Mr E.J. Beer, Mr R. Chichester, Mr Lock, Mr Morrish, Mr H. Lock, Mr J, Beer, Mr W. Beer.*

Bishops Tawton Bell ringers in around 2000.
Back row: Paul Munt, Richard Tossel, Alf Stevens, Michael Beer. Front row: Bill Prouse, Colin Tovey.

Bell ringers at Bishops Tawton 2014.
Back row: Colin Dudley, Alan Watts, Robin Runnalls, Sarah Amery, Andrew Snell, Richard Amery. Front row: Alfie Stevens, Richard Tossel, Michael Beer (captain), Michael Snell.

The tower today has six bells. The interior was smartened up in 2013 and new ropes were attached to the bells in March 2014.

The Churchyard

There is a website that records the graves in churchyards, www.gravestonephotos.com

The section for Bishops Tawton is not completely up to date but has lists and access to photos of graves stones up to the early '70s. It tells us that there were 415 graves at that time. There is information about their birth and death year as well as their age. There is extra information for a few.

A couple of interesting and very different stories follow but surely each and every grave has its own interesting life story to tell.

An academic, historian, political advisor and organic farming pioneer

Edward Jenks, buried at Bishops Tawton, was born in Surrey. His first wife died giving birth to their son who died fighting in the First World War. Edward Jenks married Dorothy Mary Forward in 1898, she was one of twelve children of Sir William Bower Forwood and Lady Mary Forwood. Edward went to Kings College Cambridge; he worked at University of Melbourne, University College Liverpool, Victoria University of Manchester, University of Oxford and University of London. He was a leading academic in relation to the English Civil War. During the Second World War War he was an advisor to an extreme right wing party and was detained in prison from 1940 to 1941. He was a pioneer of organic farming and a founder member of the Soil Association. He died in Devon in 1963.

This information is taken from the website above.

A steam engine driver

Samuel Beer was one of the most esteemed Great Western Railway drivers of his time in the area. He died in 1908 as the result of a dreadful accident and was buried in St John the Baptist churchyard in Bishops Tawton. Engraved on his gravestone is this picture of a steam train.

Samuel Beer was sixty years old and had been an engine driver for the company for many years. As was common practice, two engines were attached to the passenger train that was due to arrive in Barnstaple at 9.34pm. When the train stopped at Filleigh, Samuel stepped out onto the line in order to oil some of the machinery on the second engine. This was not common practice at that station as oiling had

The steam engine on Samuel Beer's gravestone.

Samuel's gravestone.

taken place in South Molton and would not then have been required until the train's arrival in Barnstaple. On this occasion two of Samuel's daughters and his granddaughters were travelling on the train having come from Taunton. Perhaps he wanted to leave promptly to be with them on their arrival in town.

Witnesses to the accident stated that Mr Ackland, the guard, gave the signal to the first engine to proceed, which it did without sounding the whistle. Samuel was caught on his own train and crushed. He severely damaged his arm and broke some ribs. Despite this he was able to walk and travelled on his own train to the North Devon Infirmary. The following day it was decided that his arm could not be saved and amputation took place. Unfortunately Samuel died some three hours after the operation.

This information is taken from an article written at the time in the *North Devon Journal*.

The Methodist Chapel

Bishops Tawton's first non-conformist chapel was opened in 1868. In the 1860s a few friends had got together for worship in various homes in the village. They purchased a bit of land from Mr Gould to erect a place of worship. This was in Village Street right opposite Thomas's agricultural and engineering works.

In July 1867 there was a ceremony of stone laying and afterwards they moved to a nearby field where about 100 people sat down to tea. In the evening there was a meeting in the field where people from several denominations spoke. The first Bible Christian chapel was built by a builder called Mr Stone. The music in the chapel was sustained by Mr George Thomas and his family and by George Taylor who led the singing on his flute. The chapel was opened in March 1868 and together with the schoolroom could seat 180 people. The cost of the chapel was £320. 4s. 3d. Over £200 was raised by subscriptions and collections and takings on the opening day. In those days the trustees meetings lasted all day The

ladies of the church made lunch and tea in the gallery the business part of the meeting was in a room kindly lent by the Gospel Hall.

The Sunday School was formed by Mr Barrow and was later taken on by Mr Sexon. In 1879 the school had thirty children and four teachers and in 1908 sixty-five children and twenty-four teachers.

Numbers at the chapel increased from around 15 at the start to 92 by 1907. In 1907 a new heating system and organ were added and paid for. The chapel became too small and money was raised and

The Methodist chapel today.

Below: *This shows the wedding of Walter Tonkin and Marjorie Hill. They were married at the old Methodist chapel in August 1931. Walter and Louise Tonkin are in the front row. William and Bertha Hill are also present. 'Granny Smalldon' is wearing the long dress. The bridesmaid is Edna Hill. The harmonium was played by Daisy Ford of Ford and Locks.*

the old chapel sold for £175.

Stella Beer tells us that she was the last one to be baptised there and her parents are thought to be the last ones to have been married there.

COPY OF FINANCIAL STATEMENT FORWARDED TO CHAPEL COMMITTEE

Income	£	s.	d.	Expenditure	£	s.	d.
Special Effort	330	4	8	Cost of Site (and Conveyance)	114	16	6
Subscriptions (not included in Stonelaying)	272	12	6	Architect's Fees	72	0	0
Interest from Bank	4	9	10	Builders' Account	1368	3	5
Stonelaying Day	254	0	4	Padfields's Carpets	11	9	1
Opening Day	241	16	7	Jarvis (Crockery)	2	12	3
Sale of Old Chapel	175	6	11	Printing and Hymn Sheets	1	8	0
Borrowed from Mr. Northcote	250	0	0	Interest on £250	1	17	0
Opening Sunday Collection	3	9	6				
Deficit	40	5	11				
	£1572	6	3		£1572	6	3

The financial statement at the time of the building of the new chapel.

Building the New Chapel

The trustees at that time were Rev. R. G. Wilton, W. Waldron, G. Thomas, J. Morrish, A. J. Verney, A. Morrish, W. T. Ford, A. J. Thomas, and J. Maxworthy. At a trustee meeting in 1934 it was decided that the present building had become "unsuitable and inadequate". Mr Morrish was authorised to approach Mr F Taylor concerning a piece of land by the Barnstaple Exeter road. Several pieces of land were looked at. The piece of land on the main road was purchased and plans were drawn up.

The stone laying ceremony was held on 13 April 1936. The opening day was Wednesday 30 September 1936.

The last service was held in the old chapel followed by a lunch in a marquee and then the new chapel was formally opened. The ceremony was performed by Mr Beckly. The key was handed to Mrs Beckly and she unlocked the door and led the congregation into the new building   There were so many people that the service had to be relayed to the crowds outside. The Mayor of Barnstaple Mr Manaton referred to attacks in continental countries as war clouds were already gathering.

It was built at a cost of £1400.

There was a tree and shrub planting ceremony in 1937 followed by tea and a Grand Concert in the evening given by the choir. This raised money to cover the building debts.

Sue Squire tells us that her grandfather Mr Morrish, built the Methodist chapel.

In 1953 a pipe organ was purchased for £500. The opening of the pipe organ was an important event and a whole day was organised to celebrate the event. The day finished with a sacred concert by Bideford High Street Methodist church.

The organ was about fifteen years old, it was made by a firm of organ builders in Plymouth. The organ was dedicated by the Rev. F. H. Everson, Rev. B.

The finished chapel.

The opening of the pipe organ.

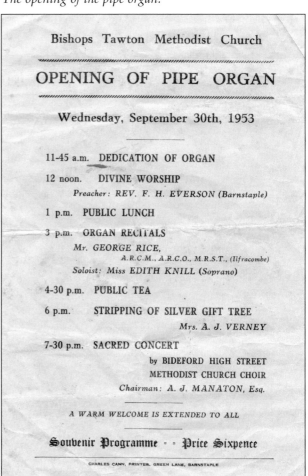

Bishops Tawton Methodist Church

OPENING OF PIPE ORGAN

Wednesday, September 30th, 1953

11-45 a.m. DEDICATION OF ORGAN

12 noon. DIVINE WORSHIP
   Preacher: REV. F. H. EVERSON (Barnstaple)

1 p.m. PUBLIC LUNCH

3 p.m. ORGAN RECITALS
   Mr. GEORGE RICE,
      A.R.C.M., A.R.C.O., M.R.S.T., (Ilfracombe)
   Soloist: Miss EDITH KNILL (Soprano)

4-30 p.m. PUBLIC TEA

6 p.m. STRIPPING OF SILVER GIFT TREE
   Mrs. A. J. VERNEY

7-30 p.m. SACRED CONCERT
   by BIDEFORD HIGH STREET
   METHODIST CHURCH CHOIR
   Chairman: A. J. MANATON, Esq.

A WARM WELCOME IS EXTENDED TO ALL

Souvenir Programme - - Price Sixpence

CHARLES CANN, PRINTER, GREEN LANE, BARNSTAPLE

The £4,000 extension to **Bishops Tawton** church, in the Plymouth and Exeter District, has been opened. The opening ceremony was the culmination of months of work by members. Mr A L Sparkes, of Braunton, unlocked the door to the new schoolroom and kitchen. The Rev Ralph Yates, of Williton, a former minister in the Barnstaple circuit, conducted the service, and the official opening ceremony was performed by the Rev D M Dobell.

After tea, the gift tree was stripped by Mrs W Feltham. Mr Wickham was chairman at the evening concert. Proceeds for the day totalled £839, which left the church free of debt over the project.

A newspaper cutting describing the celebration.
N. DEVON JOURNAL.

The opening of the extension kitchen to the Methodist chapel. Including Mr Tom Ford, Mr Lock, Mr Jack Morrish, Rev. Lawrence Smith, Rev. Ralph Yates.

BISHOPS TAWTON METHODIST CHURCH

Silver Jubilee Celebrations
1936 — 1961

Saturday, November 4th—
High Tea at 5-30, 2/6 (by ticket only)
Cutting of Cake by Mr. John Morrish
Jubilee Greetings at tea table

7 p.m. Public Meeting—
Speakers: Mr. & Mrs. David Foot Nash (Plymouth)
Chairman: A. J. Manaton, Esq.

Sunday, November 5th. 11 a.m. & 6-30 p.m.
Preacher: Mr. David Foot Nash

LOOK BACK WITH THANKS — LOOK FORWARD WITH FAITH!

A ticket for the Silver Jubilee celebrations.

P. Evans and Pastor Thompson. The first notes were played by Mr E. Jones. During the afternoon organ recitals were given by Mr George Rice. The soloist was Miss Edith Knill. There was a concert in the evening by the Bideford High Street Methodist Church Choir.

In 1962 the solid fuel boiler was replaced by an oil fired boiler.

Mr Morrish produced a plan to put a new room downstairs and a kitchen and cutting room upstairs This went ahead in 1972 at a cost of £3983.05. There was a grand opening with a big crowd of people attending.

There were big celebrations in 1961 when the chapel was twenty-five years old. The original church group were 100 years old but the chapel was twenty-five years old. Tickets were issued and a whole day of celebrations took place. A gift book was started, Bishops Tawton Society gave £50 and the Bishops Tawton Women's Guild £5, other amounts varied from 5 shillings to £25. The whole day raised £235. The Rev. Yates was the Pastor at the time. Many villagers remember him fondly during his time at

REV. RALPH YATES TO BE ORDAINED

Sheffield ceremony

The Rev. Ralph Yates, of Bishops-tawton, is to be formally ordained into the Methodist Church at their Sheffield conference next week.

Mr. Yates and his wife have lived in the Barnstaple area for the past eight years but are soon moving to a new ministry at Camborne, in Cornwall.

In 1960 he was president of Barnstaple Free Church Council, and he is now Free Church Chaplain to the North Devon Infirmary.

Representing the Plymouth and Exeter district at the conference will be Deaconess Joan Ryland, of the South Molton circuit.

A newspaper cutting tells us about the ordination of the Rev. Ralph Yates.
N. DEVON JOURNAL.

Bishops Tawton. In August 1966 there was a celebration of the organ reopening with an organ recital and supper. Among the guests were the Mayor of Barnstaple when the foundation stone was laid and Mr J. Morrish who built the church with his father.

The Gospel Hall

The Plymouth Brethren met in a building now a house called Homeleigh. They met on the upper floor and there was a saddler and boot repairer downstairs. Then they built the new Gospel Hall opposite the Chichester Arms, where it is today.

Sally Crook remembers her father was a founder member of the Gospel Hall and he helped with the building of the Hall in 1925.

Hugh Thomas remembers as many as ninety children going to the Gospel Hall Sunday School at its peak. He said,

"Sunday School was at 2pm and it enabled you to get out of the washing up which was a huge attraction and probably contributed to its success!"

Denise Webber tells us that her father was a circuit preacher for the Bethren. He used to cycle in all weathers to outlying villages. He would leave home at three o' clock in the afternoon on a Sunday for the half past six service and come home at ten o'clock, almost every week.

Lorna Holland remembers,

"We used to go to the Brethren chapel up in the village. We used to go to a club, we always liked to go there because the songs were quite jolly. We used

Homeleigh in Village Street where they met before the Gospel Hall was built.

The Gospel Hall.

to do a concert, we had to recite little pieces and sing songs at Christmas, and then we would get our Christmas present. A man I think he was called Mr Bedford, always bought us all an orange. They used to take us on trips to the beach, to Croyde and we went to Exmouth. We used to go to the Church Sunday School too but it wasn't always available. We went to the Methodists too, that's where Mr Yates did a lot for us. They did little concerts too and we played games, it was more like a youth club where you all joined in."

Sunday Schools Around the Village

Sunday School was a popular activity for children. As many people remember there was not a lot to do in the village and Sunday School provided religious instruction as well as entertainment and a place to meet friends. All three churches have had a number of Sunday Schools and clubs for children over the years.

Jean Ford remembers,

"It was a small village and there wasn't much to do so we went to the Church, Chapel and Brethren Chapel. Everyone went!"

Sue Squire remembers the Methodist Sunday School. She said, it was usual to attend two services on a Sunday. She remembers that she was not allowed to play games on a Sunday and her mother never knitted on a Sunday. Her grandmother always prepared the vegetables for Sunday on a Saturday and she never watched television on a Sunday. She remembers a Sunday School outing to Exmouth which Mr Tom Ford organised. There were too many passengers for the number of seats in the coach so some people had to sit on stools down the aisle of the bus for the entire journey both ways!

Tricia Andrews recalls her mother Mary Storey was the organist at the Methodist chapel in 1940s and '50s. She went to Sunday school there and went on Sunday School outings to places like Bude and Paignton. Brian Ford's father, Tom and Miss Morrish were Sunday School teachers. On Friday night they had the Band of Hope meetings.

Shirley Geen taught Sunday School at St John the Baptist church. There were about 30 children in the Sunday School then. She said,

"There was nothing else to do so most children went and most were well behaved."

Shirley remembers her own Sunday school experiences, a few years earlier,

" You had to wear a hat to Sunday School and if you moved when you were in church you got two fingers stuck in your back from the vicar's wife. I went to Sunday School in the morning and afternoon from

This appears to be a very old certificate for the Sunday School at the parish church, dated 1817. It shows the church before the alterations were done.

An early Sunday School group. This was taken in the grounds of Court Farm. Several children have been named, Alf Morrish, Winnie Isaac, Florrie Tanton, Wallace Smalldon, George Smalldon, Eddie Smalldon, Freddie Smalldon.

A Methodist Church Sunday School group around 1965. Some children are named, Richard Ford, Michael Ford, Johnny, Martin and Andrew Ward, Paul Shapland, Christopher and Teresa Walters.

the age of three, I had to learn a collect prayer every week and recite it and in the afternoon I had to learn a piece from the New Testament. It was a nightmare! There were teachers, two Miss Hollands, Miss Beer, Miss Cole. There were good things about Sunday School, I liked the outings and the Christmas party. I remember a Christmas party in the Village Hall, it was beautifully decorated and they had good teas provided by Mrs Lock. Towards the end they turned off all the lights and we saw the huge Christmas tree with lots of little candles lit on it. I remember the magic of that."

Do re mi fa sol la ti do, a Bishops Tawton Beginning!

John Curwen became a world famous name following his time and experience at Bishops Tawton. In the early 1830s he took up his first post as a non conformist clergyman in North Devon, at the Barnstaple Independent Chapel in Cross Street.

John Curwen.

He was a Sunday School teacher here in Bishops Tawton and while teaching the children he noted that there were many children living in the village and to quote from his letter,

"since there is a good day school there, the children are more than usually intelligent and attentive."

He worked on the Sunday School which was not so popular at the time. He began weekly services for children which were held an hour before the regular service. He soon had around one hundred children coming each week. When he, eventually, was posted elsewhere, he did not want to tell his congregation in Bishops Tawton that he was leaving. The news leaked out. On his last service the chapel was crowded with children and parents. The children conducted the service, they sang the hymns he had taught them and towards the end the children and parents began weeping. Curwen shook hands with everyone and declared that he would never forget them.

He recognised the importance of hymn singing for his Sunday School children and because he had difficulty himself reading music he became interested in Glover's method of teaching. He adapted this, made several modifications and hit on a system that later made him famous. He decided on a rhythm notation and a pitch representation system using the do, re, mi, fa, sol, la, ti, do that is familiar to us today. He went on to publish textbooks and song books through his own publishing company in London. By 1872 his methods had spread through Britain and to the far outreaches of the British Empire. In 1860 it was recognised by the English Education Department and by 1891 two and a half million children were receiving instruction in the sol fa. Many other countries also adopted it.

Herner Church

Herner church sits within the parish of Bishops Tawton.

> The *North Devon Journal* of 9 August 1888 records, *"The site of the place of worship has been admirably chosen. From Hall its gracious donors look down through the avenue, upon the tower which will eventually contain two bells. The church itself lies embosomed in the delightfully wooded valley between the Taw and the commanding eminence upon which Hall stands."*

Herner church has some of the carvings taken from an earlier medieval chapel that was attached to Hall. The need for another church in the parish was justified at the time because the hamlets around and about Hall were considered to be so far distant from the ancient church of Saint John the Baptist that

Little Hill, Cuckoo Lane, chapel at Herner.
LITTLE HILL CHAPEL. BEAFORD OLD ARCHIVE IMAGES © BEAFORD ARTS.

This is the cottage where Alfie Steven's family lived, in Cuckoo Lane, Little Hill. It was pulled down several years ago. In 1941, Alf on his mother, Bessie's, knee, Wilfred and his father Charlie Stevens. The Chapel was a little further along the road on the left.

people were unable to attend church. It is called a chapel of ease.

> It opened on 2 August 1888
> Richard Chichester's diary records,
> *"Rev. W. G. Morcom and H. Bremridge took them round the garden, we then walked to Herner and assisted Beatrice arrange seats etc in the new church. I walked down by the railway to call on H. Bakers and General J. Chichester, back to lunch at 1. 32 present. New church opened, service at 3. I read 1st lesson. Preb Pigot preached. Large congregation. Capital tea at school, 4.50. Fine."*

There was a chapel at Herner at Little Hill Cuckoo Lane. This was demolished in the late '70s or early '80s. Alfie Stevens remembers attending Sunday School here, he said there were about 20 children there each week and it ran from three o'clock in the afternoon. Tom Hartnol was a Sunday School teacher and his daughter played the organ.

The entrance to Herner church.

Chapter 7

Health, Welfare and Community

"You could sit on anyone's doorstep and you would be welcome"

Jean Ford.

Bishops Tawton, although relatively near to Barnstaple, has always promoted and held a good sense of community. Historically, long before the inception of the Welfare State, this was very important in supporting the good health and welfare of parishioners. The ability to have regular work to be able to pay for limited medical attention and to have access to nourishing food was everything. For those less fortunate, the kindness of friends and neighbours and relief through local charitable benefactors, the church and other local organisations, may have been the only way for people to cope in times of illness and unemployment.

Some Historical Facts:

Bishops Tawton, like other villages, had its own Poor House at one time for vagrants and the destitute. This was situated in the churchyard, alongside the road and had been built in 1630. The arched entrance to the churchyard we see today is a Victorian addition, the original entrance being down on the corner near the cottages. Money had been donated for the poor by wealthy local benefactors between 1602 and 1680 amounting to £59.10s. For those without money, work or a home, provision would have been through the Parish Poor House. This had been built with some of the charity money. It eventually ceased to be used following the new English Poor Laws being passed in the 1830s when larger workhouses were subsequently built in the nearest towns.

From the 1830s, Bishops Tawton people unfortunate enough to find themselves needing to be admitted to a workhouse would have been sent to Barnstaple. After the creation of the National Health Service in 1948, the old town workhouse in Alexandra Road eventually became an NHS hospital and subsequently has been rebuilt as flats though the original workhouse chapel and pattern of the original entrance arch survives.

Bishops Tawton churchyard. Today the War Memorial stands in the area where the old Parish Poor House once stood.

In 1840, the old Bishops Tawton Parish Poor House, by then between 150 and 200 years old, was pulled down. Apparently, usable materials from the building were sold to the vicar who then used them towards building a new church school – a building now somewhat remodelled but still in daily use as the Village Hall.

The churchwardens were often Overseers for the Poor and also used poor money to make provision for individuals who may have been in what was viewed at the time of genuine need of help. There is a record for example, dating from 1731, where an order was made to take care of Mr Baker of Bishops Tawton who had been "badly burnt in an accident in a kiln. The unfortunate man had been burned from knee to foot, a burn on his thigh as broad as a hand, his arm and wrist and his shoulder."

Charitable Benefactors

Until 1885, much of the Newport area, out as far as the Landkey road, used to be part of the Bishops Tawton parish. Some of the distribution of relief for the poor would therefore have covered both areas.

There is historical evidence of various benefactors providing gifts for the poor of the parish. Mostly these were financial gifts, overseen by trustees drawn from the gentlemen of the parish, to provide poor relief in perpetuity – sometimes as cash but often in the form of that most basic staple: bread. One of these, the Berryman Gift, survives today.

Berryman's Gift

In 1618 John Berryman gave the considerable sum of £100 to buy land for the poor of the parish of Bishops Tawton. In 1619, land was purchased from local landowner, the Chichester family, at Pill. This consisted of two meadows and an orchard, a total of 3¾ acres. Profits (i.e. rents) from use of that land and of two small houses on the land were to be used to benefit the poor. The parcel of land concerned ran between Pill Lane and Bishops Tawton Road, including the area around what is now Oatlands Avenue. This land became known as "The Poor Land" and since the early 1900s, it was shown as one field: OS map 4347. Trustees were responsible for the rents and were required to present annual accounts at Easter in the Church House to show how the profits had been bestowed.

From 1800, money from the Berryman Trust was distributed every third or fiurth year from the church vestry to the deserving poor. There were always large numbers of claimants, mainly labourers from the parish. Sums were allocated according to the size of families. In 1860, it is recorded that the annual rent

for the land was £10, in 1905 it was £13 and in 1965, £40. The land continued to be held by the trustees to as recently as 1998 when it had to be sold to make way for the extension of the Barnstaple bypass or link road. Much of the original land now forms part of the embankment to the new road crossing the Taw.

The original gift, along with the details of others was recorded on oak panels in Bishops Tawton church. The panels were originally attached to the front of a gallery which had been on the west wall of the church. The gallery was removed in the late 1800s but the panels were fortunately preserved and moved to the vestry.

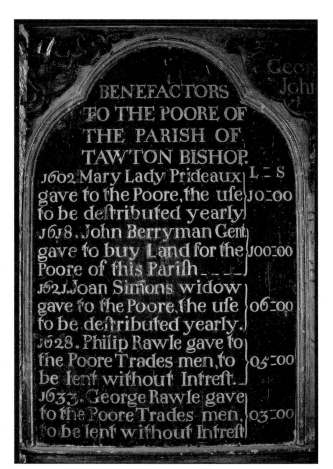

Detail from an original oak panel in the church showing the Berryman Gift.

Over the years other charitable funds were added to the original Berryman Gift which became known as known as the Berryman Trust. This included interest from the original parish poor money, some of which had been used to build the Poor House, and, later, funds from the Sanders Coal Trust and money left over when the local Nursing Aftercare Committee closed down in the 1980s – more on which is given below.

Interest continues to be distributed today through the trustees who advertise its availability. The trustees comprise of representatives from the Church, Church Council and Parish Council. Applications are invited every two years for the modest funds when any older residents who have lived in the parish for at least the preceding twelve months may apply.

Some other notable gifts for the poor also recorded on the panels:

Martyn's Gift: In 1663, Elizabeth Martin gave money for the catechizing of children forever. (This lovely old word means to teach the principles of Christian religion.) This money was £1.6s.8d a year to be paid out of Great Fisherton. It was paid to the vicar who "regularly catechizes the children at a Sunday School in the parish". In the 1800s this money was recorded as being paid by the then owner – Mr Charles Chichester.

Hugh Ackland's Gift: in his will in 1620, he left 6d a week forever to be paid in bread out of the lands of Westacott of Landkey for the poor of Newport (Newport at that time being in the parish of Bishops Tawton).

Rowley's Gift: In 1772, John Rowley gave bread annually to the poor on the feast of St John the Baptist. This continued intermittently until 1873 when it ceased, probably due to the abolition of compulsory church rates.

The three panels in the church which commemorate benefactors' various gifts to the poor of Bishops Tawton.

Bishops Tawton Benevolent and Friendly Society: January 1817 to July 1878

Long before the days of any type of national health provision or welfare benefits, all medical and nursing care had to be paid for, and no work through illness or misfortune meant there wasn't any income. This Friendly Society, like thousands of others across the

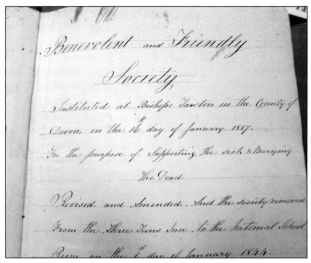

The beginning of the Bishops Tawton Benevolent and Friendly Society. N. DEVON RECORD OFFICE.

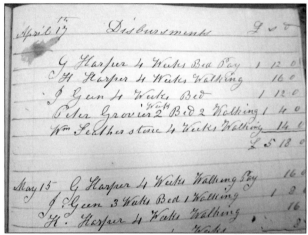

Payments made by the society in April 1878. N. DEVON RECORD OFFICE.

country, was set up to help the working classes. Members agreed to pay in a weekly or monthly sum as a type of insurance for times of sickness when they would not have been able to work and therefore, not get paid and also to help with the costs of burying the dead. The Bishops Tawton Society seems to have been set up as male only membership.

There were three classes of members in this society with people belonging to the first class paying in more as they had higher pay and could therefore afford to do so. The society was overseen by a clerk who maintained the record book of membership and money and by two stewards. A doctor, paid by the society, would certify that members' illnesses were indeed genuine and offer treatment, paid for out of the society funds. Members deemed unfit to work would then also receive a small weekly payment from the society according to their level of illness, whether "bedridden or walking" and linked to their class of membership.

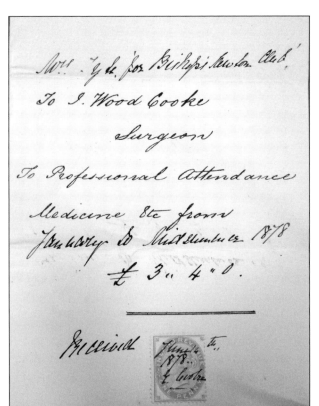

The doctor's account for services and medicines for the society. The doctor had to pay tax on his earnings with a penny tax stamp. N. DEVON RECORD OFFICE.

The popular society used to meet originally in the Three Tuns Public House which used to be in Easter Street. It moved to meeting in the National School room (now used as the Village Hall) in 1844 soon after that had been built. In 1849 there were 97 members of the Society recorded and this had risen to 158 members by 1855. By 1878 however, membership had dropped to 28 and the society closed.

Membership of these friendly societies was also another way of socialising within the community. There were annual celebrations on the anniversary of the society. In 1855 there was a particular major celebration by the Bishops Tawton Society recorded in the log book. This must have been quite a spectacle as it included a march of members through the village, probably bearing the Society flag. They marched behind a seven man band, and followed this up with beer and a meal.

The Bishops Tawton Clothing Club

This savings club had been established in the1800s to enable parishioners to save, spread the cost and pay for fabric or clothes in an era long before cheap clothing was widely available. It was linked to Wills the Drapers, a shop based in Waterloo House in Barnstaple High Street. In 1888 this club is recorded as holding the grand sum of £14.7s. and 8d. (£1 at that time would have the approximate purchasing power of about £74 in 2014).

Local savings clubs for food, fuel or clothes were quite common in the 1800s. Some were self governed and operated along the lines of the friendly societies, some set up by the retailer with perhaps a financial incentive and some were operated through the clergy, maybe such funds then being used to help buy new clothes for "Sunday best". From the account sheet shown here which was provided for the vicar, we can assume the Bishops Tawton club was linked to the church in some way. There are 56 members listed on this 1889 account sheet which had been prepared at Christmas. Possibly these represent the savings of members to use for Christmas shopping.

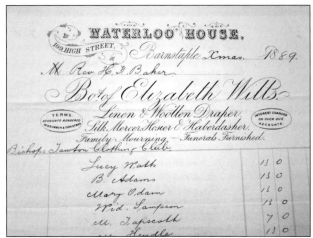

The Bishops Tawton Clothing Club.

Health of the Children

Extracts from Bishops Tawton School Log Books from 1890 to the 1940s demonstrate how much more common the spread of childhood illnesses were without the vaccinations, treatment and good public health measures we enjoy today. Though well before the inception of the Welfare State, there were some measures in place by local officers for health to help contain the spread of illnesses.

1897
Jan 22: The attendance this week has fallen off considerably. A great many children are ill – some with measles.

Feb 5: Received notice this morning from the clerk that the Medical Officer has ordered the school to be closed for a fortnight on account of an epidemic of measles among the children.

Sept 3: The attendance has been worse than ever this week. Two families have scarlet fever which prevents all the members from attending and the weather has been very wet and stormy.

In 1906 a severe outbreak of whooping cough affected the school for over three months

Aug 27: Today the school reopened. Two or three children are absent owing to their suffering from whooping cough.

31Aug: The Medical Officer of Health has instructed me to exclude those children coming from homes where there is a case or cases of whooping cough.

Sept 17: Half the school were absent. The Medical Officer of Health has ordered the school to be closed for two weeks.

Oct 15: After having been closed for four weeks school reopened today.

Oct 26: Poor attendance as several children not yet recovered from whooping cough.

1913
June 16: Mr Davie visited the school today and gave me 'recommends' for those children whom the Dr certified as having bad teeth in order that they may go to the North Devon Infirmary for treatment.

1914
Oct 20: In consequence of Gertrude Hill being ill with diphtheria the remainder of the children of that family have been excluded from school.

1918
Oct 24: More than half the scholars being absent this morning through an epidemic of influenza. The managers decided to close the school. The school was closed until Nov 11th.

1923
Nov 17: The Medical Officer of Health has ordered the school closed for a fortnight on account of a number of children suffering from whooping cough. The school remained closed till Dec 21st

1924
March 1: Closed 3 weeks – measles.

1928
April 23: One scholar away from school suffering from diphtheria all the others of the family are excluded from school.

1938
November 18: Because of a case of infant paralysis in the village, the MOH came to school and examined all the children.

1940
July 7: Ivor Smalldon died from diphtheria. The school is closed until further notice.

And a rather sad living memory from this time: *Very vividly, I remember during the war there was an outbreak of diphtheria here. The school was closed. A young boy just along New Road, from us, unfortunately died. Ivor Smalldon he was called. One or two of the other children at the school were sent to Bideford, to the Isolation Hospital. Fortunately they recovered.*

Michael Beer.

84 Children in the school subsequently received three vaccinations against diphtheria over the next 6 months but in …

1946
May 20: Dr Martin, MOH visited school and immunised a large number of children against infection from diphtheria. He was astonished that some parents would not give consent for their children to be protected.

September 9: Every child is now supplied with free milk in bottles and when one is ill, it is sent home to him.

Lorna Holland, whose mother helped at the school in the 1950s remembered her mother warming the bottles of milk by the old school coal fire on very cold mornings. The milk would always be cold in winter but sometimes would be frozen on the top and needed to be drinkable quickly as some of the children had walked a very long way into school from outlying farms and cottages.

The Law Memorial Houses

There are very few villages in the area that have their own memorial or "Almshouses". The prominent Law Memorial Houses in the main road of Bishops Tawton were built and paid for 1885 by Mary Jane Law to provide "homes for poor parish women". She had them built in memory of her husband Thomas Shephard Law who was a surgeon at the North Devon Infirmary at Barnstaple, and of her son William Henry Law who had died in 1855 at the age of twenty-nine years. It is believed that Mary lived in

The Bishops Tawton Law Memorial Houses.

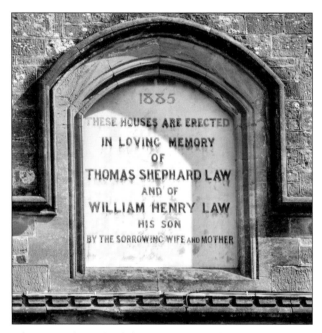

Plaque on the wall of the Law Memorial Houses showing detail of dedication by Mary to her husband and son – Thomas and William Law.

The Law Memorial stained glass window in Bishops Tawton church. The inscription at the base of the window reads: "In loving memory of dear friends who have passed from death unto life. This window is inserted by Mary Jane Law."

the Newport area which was, until the mid 1880s, part of the Bishops Tawton parish.

An extract from Mary Law's will in 1881 reads; *"Left to Charles Chichester and two others (as trustees) a piece of land – part of tithe apportionment 595 with hedge and fence separating the land from the 602 allotment field, 6 almshouses, trustees meeting room, and other buildings a trust forever to be used as almshouses with offices and gardens for the benefit of the aged or infirm poor inhabitants of the parish of Bishops Tawton or any other parish in Devon."*

Mary also left money for the keeping of a tablet on the church wall which she and her husband had erected in memory of their only child William; for two other tablets for her husband and herself; and also to pay for a stained glass window. She left money to Hugh Fortescue, Viscount Ebrington, to do this. During her lifetime, Mary reserved the right to appoint and remove alms people (residents) and trustees. But on her death, she also left instructions for the trustees of the almshouses stipulating the numbers of trustees, when they should be replaced and criteria on the selection of alms people.

At the time the houses were built, many widows or single women in the parish would have lost their rented and tied homes on retirement or on the death of their husbands. Such an opportunity of residing in an almshouse within the parish would have been highly valued. At the time of Mary's death, four of the six houses were occupied by women and two by former servants and their wives. All received a small weekly income from the trust. One of the inmates acted as bailiff. A memorial tablet to Mary Law was added to the wall in 1902.

Later in the 1900s, the six houses were changed into 12 flats. By the 1950s, residents were paying about three shillings a week in rent.

Ann Sherlock recalls that her mother-in-law lived in the Law Memorial Houses in the late 1970s. In those days, the gardens at the back were divided up and each resident had their own bit of garden for vegetables."

In 2011 following a period of extensive investment and refurbishment, the 12 flats reverted back to houses. A celebratory open day was held allowing parishioners to look around the new accommodation offered in this lovely historical building.

The Reading Room

The Reading Room, which still stands today in Village Street, had been provided by Miss Davie who lived at The Elms in the 1800s and was built by John Beer, a local carpenter and builder. The building was given for parishioners as a place to read and socialise.

An inscription on the building in stone read:
"Happy is the man that findeth wisdom, and the man that getteth understanding. For the merchandise of it is better than the merchandise of silver, and gain there of fine gold."

(Proverbs 3:13-18.)

Reading rooms were a common sight in most rural parishes in Victorian times. They were often provided by wealthy landowners or the local gentry as a philanthropic gesture and seen to be contributing to the welfare of village people by encouraging literacy. They also offered an alternative to the village inns and a social meeting place before village halls were available. Access to village reading rooms was usually through membership. Many items such as books and games were donated. A very small fee was often charged to ensure the availability of a regular

Mrs Ethel Shapland. Late of Little Fisherton. One of the residents of the Law Memorial Houses. She lived at Number 6.

The Bishops Tawton Reading Room still stands in Village Street.

A horse-drawn removal cart outside of the Law Memorial Houses belonging to Lewis Removals of Barnstaple. This picture, from the Lewis family, is thought to have been taken when moving the first residents into the Law Memorial Houses.

85

supply of newspapers, the cost of which would have been out of the reach of many.

Little is known about the membership or use of the Bishops Tawton Reading Room in its heyday. During the years of the Second World War the room was no longer in regular use for the original purpose. It was used as a home for a while, firstly by a man from the Ministry of Information and later by a Polish family of refugees who worked for the Thomas family. After this it was used as a store and until the 1980s as a venue for miniature rail enthusiasts.

The Bishops Tawton Communal Welfare League

This draft letter from 1943 was written by the secretary of a new proposed community organisation. The secretary is recorded as living at Burton Crescent, which we know to now be Burton House at the bottom of Policeman's Hill. There is no other reference to the league in the records, we don't even know if it ever got off the ground, but it may well have been the case that this league was intended to take over from the Bishops Tawton Social Welfare Committee. That committee, which had been operational during the years of the Second World War, had been formed to look after the interests of, amongst others, local evacuees.

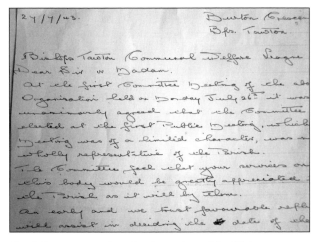

Draft letter proposing the formation of the Bishops Tawton Communal Welfare League.
N. DEVON RECORD OFFICE.

Nursing Care

Many years ago, before the introduction of the National Health Service in 1948, much of the nursing care was carried out by family, friends, neighbours, or local women who, for a small fee, would help out by going in to a home regularly or even moving in for a while to nurse the sick and the dying. People would definitely have had to pay for the services of the

professional nurse. Most parishes had a local village district nurse residing within the community in which they worked. They would also have served as the local midwife. In Bishops Tawton, money to pay for the services of the nurse was paid by parishioners into the Nursing Association Fund to help meet fees, costs of the nurses travelling and phone bills. Nurses taking up a post in a parish would most often either rent property in the village or have lodgings with someone else.

Kellys Directories from the 1930s show two nurses as residing in Bishops Tawton village over that decade:

Miss Ellen Cameron, District Nurse and State Certified Midwife (SCM) resided first at 3 Hillside and later, in 1941 was listed as living at Newlands in Chestwood.
Miss Annie Melluish, SCM and District Nurse resided at Buena Vista.

Grace Elliott can also remember a nurse living in a caravan at some time in the 1950s which was in Mr Slee's orchard behind the Bushens. It is not known if this was the qualified village nurse but she is remembered as visiting daily where needed and instructing the families on what care was required.

The Bishops Tawton Nursing Association Aftercare Committee

In 1948, twelve local ladies, including the village nurse of that time, Nurse Symonds, met in the Church Rooms to discuss the formation of a new charitable committee. It was decided that the purpose was to administer funds left over from the Local Nursing Association after the introduction of the new Health Service when District Nursing had been taken over by the County Council. The work was to be based on "discussing local cases of need in the parish where cases of illness or infirmity were known to exist." Seven local ladies were duly nominated to serve on the new committee, chosen to represent various areas in the parish. The names recorded in the minute book as being:

Miss Drummond from Herner
Miss Courtenay and Mrs Waldron representing the village
Mrs Matthews, Codden Hill
Mrs Hill, the Bridges and
Mrs Howard and Miss Morrish, Chestwood.

Other local ladies who are recorded in the minute book as having worked for this committee over subsequent years included: Mrs Kitt, Mrs Beer, Mrs Brown, Miss Farley, Miss Morrish, Mrs Howard, Mrs Matthews, Mrs Smalldon, Mrs Clements, Mrs Eastman, Mrs Sexon and Mrs Geen.

It is known that the Committee kept a list of "the elderly" for reference to help them in their work. Some small gifts of money were made to individuals but more often, gifts were of nourishing food, eggs, soup, tea, fruit, cheese, sugar and drinks such as the popular brands of Horlicks, and Bengers. Occasionally, on a doctor's advice, there may even have been a small bottle of brandy! Later, in the 1960s, chickens and hundredweights of coal were often distributed. Items were provided either weekly or monthly. An account was held in the local shops from where the grocery items were purchased and with Mr Scott the coal merchant at the Sawmills for the bags of coal.

Ladies of the committee gave freely of their time, often making visits to see people at home, presumably to sometimes take the gifts and enquire after the recipient's health. The committee continued to meet

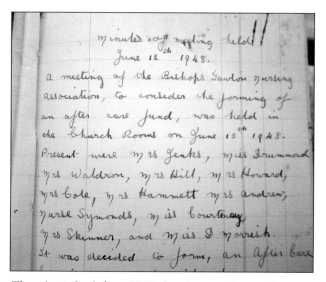

The minute book from 1948 showing creation on the new After Care Committee.

Extract from the minute book in the 1950s showing how help was distributed.

at first quarterly then twice a year from 1960 for a total of 36 years until 1984. By this time, the need for local group had diminished. This probably being a result of the growing provision of community services and other welfare benefits. The funds on closure were donated to another charity, the Berryman Trust.

Mains Services Come to Bishops Tawton

Until the early 1900s, all water used in homes was drawn from wells, springs, streams and the village tap. The water to the communal supply in the Village Square was gravity fed by a spring originating on Codden Hill. Water from the spring was held in a small reservoir in the valley towards Landkey at Codden Farm. It seems to always have been a village tap in Bishops Tawton, rather than a village pump although many individual farms and houses would have had their own pumps and wells. Water was fed in through iron pipes which eventually corroded, reducing the water to a trickle. A mains water supply was installed at the same site in the centre of the village in the 1930s as many homes still did not have their own supply at that time.

Other mains water taps were provided in roads to serve cottages and houses. Jean Ford recalls collecting water for her grandmother who lived in Glebe Cottage from a tap at the bottom of Easter Street. This was in the 1950s, the tap also serving Valley Cottages at that time. Roy Shapland can recall that in his childhood and teenage years, water for his home all had to be drawn from the well in the garden by a pump and then carried into the house in buckets. They used white enamel buckets for drinking water and galvanised buckets for washing water. It was also usual practice to use freshly collected rainwater for washing.

Contagious illnesses, some of which could be attributable to contaminated drinking water, such as typhoid, were unfortunately quite common in many parishes when there were no main drains. There was a report of a death in Bishops Tawton from typhoid fever of the daughter of Captain Davie at the Elms. Although not proven, the source of the infection was suggested to have been traced to the village tap.

Gradually, from the early 1900s onwards, houses which were built or refurbished in the village were supplied with their own mains water supply – though this may have just been a cold tap. Certainly most houses still had outside toilets, the luxury of indoor flushing toilets and bathrooms not becoming commonplace in any but the grandest homes until the 1950s or '60s.

In 1910, two old cottages in the Square were knocked down and rebuilt as three new houses. These new houses are reputed to have been the first in the village to have been built with mains water and

The "Village Square" c. late 1800s or early 1900s showing spring water being taken from the village supply.

The village tap is still to be found under the chestnut trees in 2014.

Hills View taken about 1970. The first new houses in the village to have been built (in 1910) with mains water supply.

outdoor flushing toilets. This addition was achieved apparently after some initial local opposition to such a new "modern" idea.

Bishops Tawton, like most places in England, saw significant development and a large number of properties built in the 1930s between the two wars. Building again increased after the Second World War in the 1950s and '60s. The main road through the village was widened and mains services such as gas, lighting and mains sewers installed and linked to a greater number of homes. British Gas records show that a new 6 inch mains gas pipe to the village was installed in 1939, being laid from Barnstaple along the newly widened main road which had, until the late 1920s, been just a narrow track.

Extract from Reflections: A trilogy of memories by Bert Verney.

Mains electricity also gradually came to the area in the 1930s, '40s and '50s. Bert Verney, whose family farmed at Overton, recalled in his published autobiography:

"In about 1936, my father spoke to the Electricity Company at Barnstaple, asking if it was possible to bring electricity to Bishops Tawton. They told him they could do so if they had enough people or houses which would use their power to make it worthwhile. So, father decided to canvass the whole village. You would have thought that everyone would have jumped at the chance. Not so! He had to canvass and re canvass to get enough people to get electricity installed. A few said they could not find the money but many refused to change their ways and were really afraid of electric current so said no.

In the end it made no difference, as enough people agreed and Bishops Tawton was at last lit by electricity. To bring it to our farm, half a mile from the village, we had to guarantee to pay £50 a year for 5 years. What a change! No more oil lanterns or cleaning of lamps and candlesticks … a new electric cooker indoors to replace the old range, electric cleaners

replaced the dustpan and brush and the radio ran off the mains – the days of wet batteries over."

We know Bishops Tawton with a busy main road today has bright street lighting through the whole village. Those who were children in the 1940s and '50s recall the village being very dark at night. Often the only lights that would be seen in the roads at night were lights from bicycles. Street lighting was poor and during the war subject of course to enforced blackout.

Wendy Heale, can remember that in the early 1950s there was still no electricity in the house they lived in, in South View. She remembers using candles and lighting the gas lamps; she got into trouble if the match got too short as she would damage the mantle and then the lamp wouldn't light at all.

Electrical appliances in the home were not seen until the '40s and '50s. Many people can recall getting fresh milk daily which was delivered from Court Farm by Dick Copp with Maggie the horse and cart. Until the 1960s, when milk started to be bottled on local farms, it was ladled out of the churn into your own can or jug. Most people did not have refrigerators until the 1960s or 70s.

There are some anecdotal memories of healthcare in the village from local people:

"There was also a Mrs Nutt in the village who delivered babies and laid out the dead. She lived in a red brick house past the Chichester Arms. She was known as being fierce but kind"

Shirley Geen.

"My sister Jean grabbed a carving knife from me once and I had a bad cut on my hand. A doctor lived in Easter Street, Dr Livingstone Thomas I think he was called. The house was on the left as you go down, called Angortha. (Now Fern Cottage). He treated my sister."

Cyril Dennis.

"There was the story of a midwife, who apparently used to drink a lot, they said she would always turn up having had a drink! She used to live somewhere at the back of the village."

Lorna Holland.
(Authors note: it is not known whether this was the official nurse or an unqualified local person!)

"I looked after an elderly blind lady in the Law Memorial houses for about eleven years. I would go up to help her; I went for about an hour every day. I would also send her Sunday dinner up to her. I was recommended to her family by the lady from the Post Office, that is often then what happened in those days, someone would be looking for help and you could be recommended."

Megan Runnalls.

"I remember my brother being very poorly in hospital with meningitis. The doctor at the hospital had to phone my mum at Ford and Lock's shop because we didn't have a phone. The shop was about the only place that had one so they had to pass on a message for mum."

Lorna Holland.

Cyril, Jean and Wendy Dennis pictured outside Springfield Cottages in 1947.

After the Second World War Bishops Tawton was again a growing village with quite a lot of new houses. In the post-war years there was a huge need nationally for new houses, partly to help those who had returned from war and also to improve the housing for many growing families who were living in smaller cramped and old fashioned cottages many still without bathrooms and indoor sanitation. It had been the norm that everyone used all of the rooms in their houses. Accommodation was expensive and many households took in lodgers.

The post-war building included a considerable number of brand new council houses.

Cyril Dennis recalls the move for his family to a new house, he remembers his father going up late in the evening after work to clean the new house in order that the Dennis family could be the first to move in the following morning:

"We lived in quite poor circumstances in one of the small cottages at Springfield; the cottage at that time like most of the others was really only one room down and one proper bedroom up. We children were sleeping in the landing area. My sister had tuberculosis (which was quite common in those days) which made it even more difficult. We were the first family to move into the new houses at Park Villas. They were called Park Villas as they were built in the park, part of The Elms. A compulsory purchase I think it was. We moved in 1950. My father had kept an allotment for vegetables in the field where Mount Pleasant is now to help feed us but our new house had a good garden attached."

Grace Elliott, nee Ensor, also remembers one of the benefits of moving into one of the new houses:

"I can remember when we moved in my auntie saying she had run a bath for me and it was the nicest thing I ever had. Down at my grannies, I had only been used to a tin bath, the girls had gone in first and then the boys. I also had my own bedroom with my sister, the nicest feeling."

At first, Park Villas was just built as a crescent of houses. Before the bungalows were built at the front,

The first new houses built at Park Villas taken in 1950.
N. DEVON ATHENAEUM COLLECTION, N. DEVON RECORD OFFICE.

local children would use this grassy area as a playing field. Jean Ford and Lorna Holland remembered having big bonfires and firework displays at Park Villas every year. Local children would spend a lot of time going round the village collecting newspapers and wood for the fire.

Supporting the Community

There was still a very strong sense of community in the parish in the post-war years, both through well supported village events and groups, individuals and the fostering of community effort through schools and Sunday Schools.

Bishops Tawton Methodist church seemed to be particularly busy in this respect under the guidance of the well respected Reverend Yates who lived at the Methodist Manse in the village at Cranford, in Chestwood. Sunday school children from the '50s and '60s remember taking lightings, food packages and small gifts around the village, particularly to the people living in the Law Memorial Houses.

Sue Squire (Née Brown) recalls that her Grandfather, Mr Jack Morrish supplied lightings and also delivered gifts around the village himself:

"My Granfer (Mr Morrish) was one of the most generous people I know. He would supply all the old ladies of the village with lightings, kindling,

especially those living in the Almshouses. He would go off with his car loaded and spent days delivering to them. Every Christmas he would deliver a chicken for them so that they could be sure of having poultry on Christmas Day."

Every Christmas Mr Yates would take the children from the Sunday School and Junior Guild into the Children's Ward of the North Devon Infirmary to sing and to take little gifts for them.

Access to equipment for nursing or helping the ill or frail was not always easy to get hold of, much of it being sourced by charitable means. The very active Bishops Tawton Womens Institute often put their skills to good use to fundraise for good causes such as the Red Cross. This charity, as it still does today, played an important role in the supply and loan of equipment.

Occasionally someone in need turns up at the church. Robert Sherlock recalled a day some time ago when he found someone sleeping in the church porch:

"One morning I went to open the church and I found a tramp in the porch. When I got back home and told my wife about it she asked what I had done for him. I said "I did nothing". She told me to go back with some coffee and sandwiches for him. When I looked at the visitors book sometime later, there was a nice note there signed in a very illiter-

Children from the Methodist Sunday School at Christmas, delivering lightings and carol singing to older people within the village in the 1950s. Names are: Lorna Hutchings, Colin Hutchings, Jean Lock, Margaret and Brenda Nutt, Kenneth Smalldon, Michael Braunton, Jackie Atwood, Christine Attwood, Jill, Peter Ley, Delia Braunton, Jean Nutt with the Rev. and Mrs Yates.

Sunday School children deliver crocuses to residents of the Almshouses. N. DEVON JOURNAL.

Bishops Tawton Methodist Church Junior Guilders sort packets of seeds that they will be sending abroad. February 1964. EXPRESS AND ECHO.

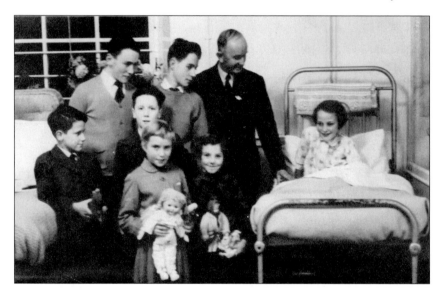

Methodist Sunday School children delivering presents to the children's ward at the old North Devon Infirmary. Circa.1960. From Left: Robin Runnalls, Graham Hockridge, Colin Hutchings, Stuart Clements and Rev. Yates. The two girls at the front are Lorna Hutchings (now Holland) and Susan Brown (now Squire). NORTH DEVON JOURNAL.

Taking the initiative: A local group of teenagers got together in the 1980s to form the Bishops Tawton Freewheelers and hold a fundraising event to buy a wheelchair for Miss Isaac who was a much loved long-term resident of Westacott Cottages. In the picture are; Grace Elliott overseeing things, Mabel Clarke, Dudley Elliott at the back, Jonathan Lean, Steven Holland is the child at the front, Katie Elliott, Scott Wells, Andrew Snell, Adam Buckingham and Shaun Holland.

ate hand saying "and I do thank that kind gentleman who brought me breakfast this morning"!

Here is a wonderful picture taken in Bishops Tawton Village Hall, probably in the 1950s or early 1960s. It was definitely taken well before the hall underwent refurbishment in the 1980s. The main entrance door was still in the centre of the end wall. No one has been able to identify the exact occasion but the consensus is that it was probably a meal provided for the older citizens of the parish to celebrate some national event. A lot of work by local ladies had been undertaken to carefully lay tables and produce what looks like many plates of ham, piles of bread and butter and fruit salad. Certainly the

hall is full to capacity. With help, we have been able to establish the identity of quite a few of those present.

With easy transport and access to the internet, the number of clubs and activities run in the village has declined overall. However, in 2014, when going to print, Bishops Tawton has three churches, a thriving pre-school group, a growing primary school, a Community Allotment Association, very active Scouts, and a community ladies group. Many other social and charitable events are held in the two village pubs and other one-off events are organised such as the popular New Year's Day walk to the top of Codden Hill.

The Community Lunch: people identified in this picture are named as follows left to right. Standing at the back and presumably serving the meal: unknown, Mrs Burgess, Mrs Facey, unknown, unknown, Mrs Knight, Mrs Facey, Mrs Beer, Miss Gibbs, Katie Balman. Seated back row from L: unknown, unknown, unknown, unknown, Alice Burrows, unknown, Mrs Maud Parker. First row from back: smiling lady unknown, Mrs Sharland, unknown, Mrs Nutt, Mr Nutt, Mrs Hammett, Mr Hammett, unknown, unknown. Second row: Miss Cope, unknown, unknown, unknown, Mrs Hanford, Mr Hanford, unknown, Mrs Day, Mrs Lewis, Mr Lewis. Third row: Miss Jenks, unknown, Miss Verney (standing) Miss Linscott, Mrs Runnalls, Mr Runnalls, Mrs Isaac, Mr Isaac. Fourth row front of photograph: Mrs Tossell, Mrs Fursdon, Mrs Moody, Mrs Beer, Mr Beer, unknown, Mr Lock, unknown, unknown, unknown, unknown, Mr Maunder, unknown.

Chapter 8

Pastimes and Celebrations

"Everyone knew everyone back then."

Jean Ford.

Over the years the community has taken part in numerous activities. There was a strong WI, drama group and a choir. Music and dancing has always been popular in the Village Hall. The hand bell ringers have entertained many parishioners over the years. Garden Shows have taken place over many years and more recently there have been allotment events. Royal occasions were a reason to celebrate too. There have been a multitude of fêtes in many venues and for many fundraising causes. The meeting of the Hunt outside the Chichester pub attracted the crowds and is a memory from the past. There is a strong history of the Scouting movement in the village with many memories to support it.

People made their own entertainment and didn't travel far, all these activities seem to be remembered as bringing huge amounts of laughter and fun. Many people volunteered their time and energy to make these things happen for others, individuals spent hours of organisation and time on small committees. There was a strong sense of community.

Girl Guides and Boy Scouts

Bishops Tawton has long had an active group of boys and girls in the Scouting movement.

There was a barn at Court Farm that was used for a Scout hut before the present one was built at the foot of Codden Hill.

Mavis Eastaugh (previously Mckeever), remembers that she moved back to Bishops Tawton in 1976, she had coffee with Marie Sexon and some how agreed to become a Cub Scout Leader. She ended up as the Deputy County Commissioner for leader training. In 1976 she began with four groups of six and a waiting list of children wanting to be Cubs too. During her time as a leader the cubs moved from the barn at Court Farm to the new hut. Mavis said,

"There was terrific support from the village, you felt it was a village."

Gwen Rider remembers the proud moment that the first Beaver Colony started in Bishops Tawton in March 2003. She watched them progress through their badge work during their hikes, craftwork, district parades, competitions and swimming. She

Bishops Tawton Cubs help to cut the grass in the churchyard 1982.

In 1982 the Cubs attended a day at Bicton and came 3rd out of 136 groups.

Marie Sexon was the Cub Leader. Marie remembers the dedication of the flag. She said the church was full at the service after the ceremony.

The first Beaver Scout Colony. Brandon Baxter, Peter Dawson, Tom Clark, Darcy Webb, Danielle Scott, Harry Brace, Elliot Parkhouse, Kris Hayward (Willow), Gwen Rider (Cherry) Beaver Scout Leader.

The re-formed Scout Troop January 2004. Alex Burnside, Jack Gordon, John Dallen, Robert Short, Rebecca Rider, (first Girl Scout in Bishops Tawton), Callum, James Burnside, Josh Smith, ?, Matthew Rider, Norman Rider, (skip), Rob Mackay, Colin, Kevin Derham.

Below: Scouts and Guides holding the colours as part of the celebration of the opening of the new area in the Methodist chapel. Julie Parkhouse and Jean Ford are two of the children and it is dated around 1960.

Below: Bishops Tawton Girl Guides in the 1950s. Muriel Allen, Angela Cooper, Maureen Beer, Margaret Houle, Marcia Copp, Mary Beer, Christine Cook, Pat Braunton, Eileen Rook, Dianne Gilbert, Shirley Rogers. They met in the Methodist church.

A certificate showing Christine Cook obtained her Child Nurse Badge as a Bishops Tawton Girl Guide.

January 1990. Some faces are recognised. Mark King, Adam Hall, Stephen Dibble, Tom Brailey, Nick Tyrell, Stephen Anderson, Daniel Oliver and James Wright.

has seen them move up through Beavers, to Cubs, to Scouts and some on to become Leaders too.

Jean Ford remembers being a Girl Guide in Bishops Tawton.

"We took sausages to the quarry to cook. We went tracking around the village. Grace Ensor (Elliott) was the Guide Leader. I remember Grace leaving early one day because she had met this nice chap called Dudley!"

The Scout Troop was revived in 1994 when seven scouts were invested. They were led by John Plowman. The Scouts and Cubs took the Santa sleigh around the village on Christmas Eve to wish the residents of the village happy Christmas and to deliver sweets to the children.

Norman Rider remembers going to camp in 2004 at Snapper. They built a rope bridge over the river with the Scouts learning about knotting rope. One Scout, a girl, was very anxious about walking across but decided to try. Unfortunately she fell in the river. She came back and tried again with other Scouts shouting fall in, fall in, and she fell in. She really didn't want to do this again but didn't want to be beaten by it. This time the Scouts were behind her

and cheering her on. She made it!! It was a good memory of teamwork and perseverance. He recalls the wonderful support from parents during the camp.

Women's Institute

Bishops Tawton WI was formed two years before the Second World War and there were eight founder members. Here are some examples of their activities, a lampshade making demonstration, a handicraft competition, a yeast cake competition and an arrangement of autumn leaves and berries.

Cynthia Snowden (née Reed) remembers being very active in the WI. She was the captain of a WI quiz. She won a competition for the best design of Christmas card in 1947. She was a member of the WI Choir and had a lead in a WI drama group farce called *The Bathroom Door* by Gertrude Jenkins. She remembers wearing a silk dressing gown, pyjamas and carrying a loofah. This was performed at the WI concert in 1948. She also conducted three items by school children at that concert, one percussion and two singing.

Above: *This shows the WI group in Bishops Tawton Village Hall. It was clearly a popular activity.*

Left and below: *WI productions.*

A WI production.

WI Drama

For several years there was a very keen group who put on productions in the Village Hall. They remember having so much fun practising, others, who were part of the audience, recall the humour too!

Sally Joy tells us that Mrs Eve was in charge and wrote the scripts. She says she was a very talented lady. Sally's mother made most of the props and Mavis Courtenay painted the scenery. They often rehearsed in Mrs Hill's lounge. There was a good supply of dressing up clothes mainly from jumble sales and with a bit of imagination and a sewing machine they were made to fit the bill.

Shirley Geen remembers,

"There was a drama group. It was mad but we loved it. I think we did one every year. One year there was a competition at Combe Martin and we did part of Mid Summer Night's Dream and some of the fairies were a bit plump, two of them were pregnant!"

Sally Joy remembers performing the play at other places too,

"We arrived at the village hall to perform for Kings Nympton. We were shown the dressing room, it had no floor! It was being renovated and we had to balance on joists and there were trenches everywhere. There were no toilet facilities but they told us they had put a bucket under the stage if anyone gets desperate! Mum started to assemble the spinning wheel and dropped the nut that fastened on to the axle. It went into one of the trenches. I kept looking to see if I could find the blessed nut when my hand touched something furry, Oh, horror of horrors it was a dead rat! I soon jumped out of that trench I can tell you."

The Choir

Members of the WI Choir are listed as, M. Skinner, W. Mc Gill, D. Walters, P. Edwards, M. Chapman, P. Parsloe, I. Palfreyman, W. Hallum, D. Gubb, B. Worth, B. Hooper, M. Jenkins, S. Jenkins. The conductor was R. Birchall.

Dancing

Dancing has always been a popular activity in the Village Hall.

Shirley Geen remembers there was an old time

The Bishops Tawton Dance Club.

dance club in the Village Hall in about 1954. She went with Les before they were married.

"Mr and Mrs Dunn started it, they ran them in lots of villages around here. The Littles from Newport took it on after that. People came from all around, some from Chapelton. Les and I went to Swimbridge to dance on Saturday nights."

Janet Law remembers old time dancing in the Village Hall in the early 1950's. A crowd of chaps would come from Atherington and High Bickington on their bikes as well as quite a few from Barnstaple. It was held once a week and Mr Wilf Dunn used to come from Goodleigh and give us dance lessons.

Sally Crook remembers dances in the Village Hall in the 1980s They were organised by Richard Tossel. There was a band called the Haymakers who played country and western music. The dances were very popular and people came from as far away as Lynton. The hall would be full, everyone was on the dance floor. There was a bar from the Three Pigeons and a supper was offered. Everyone got dressed up in those days.

Hand Bell Ringers

In 1991 the hand bells were rediscovered in the belfry at the church. Funds were raised and the bells were repaired. There have been hand bell ringers in Bishops Tawton for longer than anyone can remember. The bells are about 200 years old and were probably cast by Robert Wells of Wiltshire. There are twelve bells and they are made of copper and tin. At one time Mr Howard had a group of hand bell ringers who rang a set of bells that belonged to him. There is a record of them taking part in a concert in Braunton in 1962.

More recently John Carvosso decided to try and get the bells going again. Money was raised and the bells were restored. Several people joined the group of hand bell ringers and they had some help learning the skill from ringers in other parishes. The group have entertained many people in several locations, in the church, at coffee mornings, at WIs, weddings, garden fetes, in care homes and at the Children's Hospice.

Carnival Floats

Carnival floats were designed and made in Bishops Tawton over several years. There was a Bishops Tawton Carnival as well as floats entered by the village in the Barnstaple Carnival. Many were organized by the WI and others by the Scouting group.

The hand bell ringers. Pam Rayner, Trish Prescott, Janet Mcdonald, Jenny Stevens, Diana Nichols, Anita Lethbridge, Elvie Snow and Mary Monk.

The Mad Hatter's Tea Party.

The Carnival Queen! N. DEVON JOURNAL.

Above left: *A WI Carnival float.* Above right: *The Cubs' Carnival float outside the Village Hall in 1977. Nick Guy and Christopher Hodges can be seen on this one.* Below left: *A Viking Ship. The Cubs' carnival float in 1979.* Below right: *The Minstrels. A WI carnival float.*

Village Fêtes and Celebrations
Tawton House Fêtes

There seem to have been fêtes in the village every year. Many were in the grounds of Tawton House, which has a history of its own. It used to be two cottages, one of cob and one of stone until an adjoining room bought them together under one thatch. It has many interesting features.   There are ancient dairy tiles in the bathroom depicting religious scenes. In the airing cupboard there is a faint residue of sticky labels that indicate where the small sheets and the maids' sheets should be stacked. There was a large number of staff employed at the house. Ivy Lock worked there – she started as a maid and progressed to being the cook. She worked there from around 1914 to around 1940. The owner of the house worked away in India and at one time bought his Indian servant home to Bishops Tawton. He taught Ivy to make curries using all the spices from India. Mrs Leaworthy also worked there; she was the wife of George Leaworthy whose portrait hangs in the Village Hall.

Sally Colwell remembers the Jenks sisters liking

Tawton House in the snow.

The staff at Tawton House.

A fête in Tawton House in 1955 in aid of the church. People recognized are Mrs Smalldon, Mrs Noble, with two daughters, Tina and Paula. Mavis Courtenay and Mary Courtenay. Joan Knight with Martin and Steven. John Kelly and John Salisbury. FROM NDJ ATHENAEUM COLLECTION N. DEVON RECORD OFFICE.

This picture shows an early fête held in the grounds of Tawton House. In the front is Mrs Eileen Knight with Alan Knight in the top hat. The lady with the long black dress is the vicar's wife, Mrs Nicholas. It is dated 1947.

Country dancing at Tawton House. Terry Jones, Ian Taylor, Christine Shapland, and Ann Lavercombe.

Bishops Tawton Brownies maypole dancing at the fête in the garden of the Old Vicarage. At this time the Brownies were led by Julie Down.

A fête in the Methodist church.
N. DEVON ATHENAEUM COLLECTION
N. DEVON RECORD OFFICE.

An early celebration at The Elms. This is well before Park Villas were built looking up towards the house.

A group of ladies celebrating at Ford Gate. Mary Beer,?, Mrs Ridd, Mrs Vera Lock, Mrs Beer, Mary Swain, Winnie Huxtable, Vera Huxtable, Mrs Hopper, Mrs Swain, Mr Hopper, Mrs Bessie Smith.

Morris dancing outside the Chichester Arms.

A fête in the Village Street. The Brownies performing.

children to go and play in their garden; there were toys, a swing a hammock and a sandpit.

Meg Runnalls remembers every summer there used to be a fête in Tawton House, She said,

"Miss Jenks lived there then. We would go up there on a Saturday afternoon: there were races organised for the children, games and stalls."

Jenny Stevens remembers during a fête they went to the Village Hall and there was a skittles game. The winner won a pig. This was a real live pig!

Fêtes held in many places around the village over the years. Some were held in the Vicarage garden, some at Hall, there is a record of one at The Elms, and another at Ford Gate. Some were held at Court Farm and others more recently in the Village Street. The Methodist church had fetes and there were celebrations in the Village Hall

In more recent years the Village Fêtes have been held in the Village Street with Morris dancing and stalls.

Royal Occasions

In 1956 the Queen came through Bishops Tawton on her way to plant a tree at Lapford. This was a time of celebration and several people remember it clearly. Jean Ford remembers that the school children took chairs out and waited for the car to come by. There were free flags at the shops and everyone waved to the Queen.

Grace Elliott remembers the traffic going through the village very slowly, she was a Brownie and was allowed to stand at the front.

Cyril Dennis remembers the Coronation in 1953, he went to the Waldron's house as they were the only ones he knew who had television.

The Golden Jubilee in 2002 was a time to celebrate. Funding was secured from the Tarka Country Millenium Awards. There were three parties organised for the children. In the evening a beacon was lit on Codden Hill to join in with many others being lit all around the country. There was a Jubilee Fête in the Stanley Verney Playing Field with five-a-side football competition, stalls, a BBQ and bar. There was an arts and crafts fair in the Village Hall which was part of the North Devon Festival. There was a senior citizens' party too.

Michael Snell remembers the wedding of Prince Charles and Lady Diana,

" We had a great day at L'Anne and Richard's with lots of children from both terraces. We didn't see much of the wedding but we certainly celebrated it!"

Top: *The Silver Jubilee Fête. A group walking along Village Street.*

Above: *A village celebration of the wedding of Charles and Diana.*

Below: *This was recorded in the School Log Book.*

5.56. *The Queen drove through Bishops Tawton today on her way from Barnstaple to Exeter. The children stood outside the school as the Royal car passed slowly.*

'Save Our Hall'

The Village Hall was previously the Church Hall. In 1974 a public meeting was called to discuss the state of the hall. Each group that met there sent representatives and the meeting was well attended. It was considered to be unsafe by the surveyor. It was closed by the vicar at the time and the organisations in the village had to relocate or close down. A fundraising committee was formed with representatives of all the users of the premises. A few years later Rev. Andrew Jones arrived and the hall was handed over by the Church to the village in trust. Many years of fundraising followed with many events. There was an Edwardian Fayre and others with a Wild West, Victorian, International, Musical, Gypsy, Old English and Story Land theme; each one had stalls and side shows decorated in keeping with the theme.

By 1977, the Silver Jubilee celebration, the Save Our Hall Committee had raised £1000. In 1985 after fourteen years of campaigning, applying for grants and further fund raising and a lot of worry by the committee the necessary money was raised. A new look building was opened at a cost of £40,000. It was a huge and prolonged effort by many people but built a sense of community in the village.

Chris Morrison remembers sleeping in Court Farm field to oversee the equipment set up ready for the fête event the following day.

One event on that day was a tug of war. Many people remember this with amusement.

The Lads and Lassies

Margaret Jenkins remembers,

"In 1968 the Bishops Tawton WI held a Midsummer Fair in Waldron's field. I decided to see if I could find enough children in the village interested in forming a small jazz band. I enlisted the help of the school to inform the children and took names of those who wanted to join. I visited the parents of those on the list to seek their permission. There were about twenty in number. Mr Clements the Headmaster lent me four small drums and the pastor of the Methodist chapel gave me a wonderful Boy's Brigade Drum he had played as a boy. I bought metal Kazoos for the rest of the children. We met for the first four weeks in our living room concentrating on learning the music. They liked the tune Come Lassies and Lads so we decided to make it our signature tune and adopt the name for the band from this. We practiced marching. I was giving great thought to what the children would wear. An order for 40 yards of material was sent off. We bought red taffeta to make pillbox hats for both girls and boys, we also made bows. We cut up

white sheets to make long trousers for the boys and we had enough ribbon to sew down the sides of the trousers. The material arrived and the instructions were to wash before we used it. So she put it in the washing machine but on lifting the lid there was no fabric to be seen, there was a small hard ball at the bottom, the missing 40 yards! We opened up the ball and were eventually able to use it.

The uniform was at last completed and we were so proud to see how splendid our Lads and Lassies looked as they led the parade. After this we entered them in several carnivals, they took first prize at Braunton and were treated to a fish and chip supper."

A man's competition at Court Farm. Was this the knobbliest knees or the hairiest legs? George Shapland, Michael Beer, Richard Tossel, Chris Morrison, George Jenkins, George Parkhouse and John Hopkins.

The Garden Show

There has been a Garden Show in Bishops Tawton for many years but no one seems to know when it first began. It seems to have changed from mainly a flower show to a vegetable and flower show with an element of craft and photography. In the early years it was a little later in the year to allow for the plants to be at their best; now it seems to fit in with the best vegetable harvesting time.

Alan Knight remembers his father, Leonard Knight growing many chrysanthemums for the show;he said the show was a little later in the year then so that the flowers would be in full bloom and the flower section was much bigger. He remembers helping to carry the flowers over to the hall. He remembers it was always a battle with Mr Bob Squire

Above: *The Garden Show in the early '50s.* N. DEVON ATHENAEUM COLLECTION N. DEVON RECORD OFFICE.

Right: *The Garden Show 1953.* N. DEVON ATHENAEUM COLLECTION N. DEVON RECORD OFFICE.

and Mr Daniel Beer. Mr Beer was a dahlia specialist.

Penny Rogers remembers when she was a child she presented the bouquet at the end of the show.

Patricia Andrew remembers the Garden Show and says her father Bill Slee always entered.

In there '50s there was a newspaper report about the show. The headline was "Four trophies awarded at Bishops Tawton Show". The Flower Show was opened by the president of the Allotment Society, Mr W. T. Ford. The cup for the most points in the flower classes went to Mr L. A. Knight. Mr R. Wrafton won the vegetable class cup. The fruit section was won by Mr W. T. Slee and the women's section was won by Mrs A. Squires.

Children won prizes too – the lucky ones were Jackie Moyaham and Graham Hutchings.

Gardening is a popular activity in the village. The allotments were set up as a self governing association. All the initial work was done by the group, clearing the field, fencing and dividing up plots. The allotment field has a good community feel and there is lots of enthusiasm for growing vegetables and flowers but also for enjoying the view and being outside. There have been several open days with music, Morris Dancers, steam engine, pony and trap rides and the Pick of the Crop Music Festival. Each event has been well attended and enjoyed by all.

Preparing the allotment field.

The allotment open day.

The Meeting of the Hunt

Early hunting for sport was for royalty and their nobles, those having the most leisure time and wealth. Hunting increased as transport improved. The railways made it easier for people to travel outside cities to hunt and wealthy industrialists took up hunting. There was a decline in hunting during the two world wars. In 1978 otter hunting was banned in the UK. There has been much debate and legislation about hunting over recent years with a lot of discussion about its effect on the local rural economy and the effect of increased deer and foxes on the countryside. In February 2005 The Hunting Act came into force making hunting of foxes, hare, deer and mink with dogs illegal in England and Wales. There is still parliamentary talk of overturning the ban from time to time.

It was traditional to see the scarlet-clad riders with hounds on Boxing Day and other winter days gathering outside the Chichester Arms in Bishops Tawton. Children and adults met together to watch the occasion. Trays of drinks were bought out from the pub. People remember the general noise and mayhem of the meet.

Jean Ford remembers her father had a big coat with lots of internal pockets and he used to come home with items for the family in his pockets. Sometimes mushrooms, a rabbit, a pheasant or anything else he had found.

Lorna Holland, Sue Squire and Colin Hutchings with the hounds from the hunt around 1963.

Left: *An Old picture of Bishops Tawton Hunters, they appear to have been 'rabbiting'.*

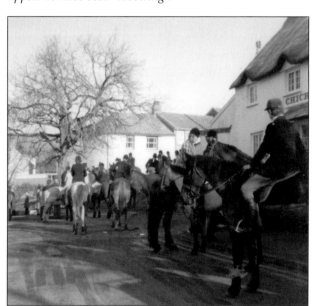

The hunt outside the Chichester Arms.

The gathering of the hunt.

Bonfire Night

Bonfire Night was another celebration time in Bishops Tawton.

Cyril Dennis remembers a big bonfire at the bottom of Codden Hill where the Scout hut now stands. They used to go to Parsons Copse, a small wood in Sentry Lane on the left and cut down trees and drag them back behind their bikes to build a massive bonfire.

Bill Bab remembers going up Sentry Lane and going to the bottom of Codden Hill to cut down trees. He and friends would get whatever they could find and tie bundles of sticks on to the back of their bikes with bits of baler cord and drag the wood back to the village. He said that,

"Over the days and weeks before the night people used to say, I got so and so for the fire, and we used to go round and collect it and put it underneath the fire."

Lorna Holland remembers all the children building a bonfire. She says, *"We used to leave the middle hollow. They used to collect newspapers all around the village with a trolley. It had the old wheels off a pram. We put everybodys' newspapers in the middle of the fire. Some of the older boys used to sleep in the bonfire for the last few nights so nobody set it on fire too early. Mrs Rice used to do hot dogs and soup. It was a really good village activity."*

Bus Trips

Bus trips were popular for many village organizations over the years. There have been a wide range, from Sunday School days out, to a holiday trip to Jersey. The holiday trip was organized by the Three Pigeons.

There have been many fund raisers – in fact most events seem to have had a fund raising cause behind them.

Bishops Tawton Mystery Tour organized by Mr Wyborn in around 1958. Jean Edwards, Jenny Smart, Dorothy Smart, Jack Hancock, Ursula Edwards, Diana Smart and David Edwards.

More fund raisers! A coffee morning in aid of Devon Air Ambulance at Whitemoor Farm. In 2006. Shirley Geen, Elvie Snow, Diana Jones, Pat Bell, Greta Harper. Dorothy Harper, Sarah Oram, Ruth Fewings, Hazel Hall, Alfie Stevens, Jenny Stevens, Gill Snow, Stella Beer, Diana Nicholls and Pat Parkhouse.

Fund raising coffees at Whitemoor Farm in the sunshine in 2007.

Chapter 9

Sport from the Past

"In their own sphere Bishops Tawton have covered themselves in glory, unbeaten champions of the third division of the North Devon League."

Quote about the village football team
from *North Devon Journal.*

Bishops Tawton Village has had many sporting successes; there have been football teams, cricket sides and badminton teams in the past. There was so much enthusiasm for the teams. Now with easier transport and a wide range of leisure activities available, including TV, there are no football, cricket or badminton teams in the village. Times have changed, zumba, pilates and yoga provide exercise opportunities.

Football

Football has been around for a long time. These dates and facts may help to put our village history into a national picture. In 1280 there is an account of a, "kicking ball game" in England. In 1526 Henry VIII ordered a pair of football boots for the "Great Wardrobe". The first official International Match took place between England and Scotland in 1873. The Football League was created in 1888. Fairly soon after this we have our first pictorial evidence of football in Bishops Tawton. The village has had an active and popular football team for many years. The early pitch was in the field adjacent to Court Farm. Later games were played in Rock Park in Barnstaple.

The earliest picture of a football team in Bishops Tawton goes back to 1907.

This old photo shows the team in 1909-10 season. On the back it says "Bishops Tawton Amateur Football Club occupies the 6th position in the North Devon League. Their record is matches played 20, won 7, total number of points 19. H. Webber, Captain. C. Neill Vice Captain. I. Smalldon & H. P. Dart joint Hon. Secretaries.

This is thought to be the village team holding the Braunton Challenge Cup. All players were awarded a medal with the date on it. Charlie Jones, Walter Cook, Charlie Turner, Fred Cook, Herbert Taylor, Rev. Nicholas, are recognised here.

The runners up in the Holman Cup 1927. Walter Cook third from left, around 1927.

This was presented to Walter Cook, Christine Shapland's father, as one of the runners up in the Holman Cup in 1927. The Holman Cup was established in 1924 and is still competed for today. The final is played at Holman Park Lynton.

Another Bishops Tawton team after the match. Bill Blackmore, Jack Nutt, S. Ley, B. Snow, B. Ensor, Lloyd Parker, Jack Brooks, D. Lock, Taylor.

Douglas Lock and Jim Symons were part of this team.

Bishops Tawton football team, 1949-50. Recognised here are Jim Symons, Douglas Lock and Bob Mellows.

EXTRA TIME
Bishops Tawton Win Braunton Cup

Bishops Tawton champions of the Third Division of the North Devon League and unsuccessful Devon Junior Cup semi-finalists, gained a second trophy on Saturday, winning the Braunton Challenge Cup with a goal scored during extra time against Lynton Reserves, whom they beat 2—1.

The final at Braunton Park was sparsely attended, gate receipts being about £10. Play lacked thrills and constructive football. Helped by the wind, Lynton attacked for long periods but were held in Bishops Tawton's defence. Right-back Nutt was always prominent. Bishops Tawton settled down and Connor turned to account a smart pass from Meadows. Lynton centre-forward Jones who had missed narrowly twice before, equalized a few minutes later.

The second half was fairly even for a time, but Lynton controlled the ball better and towards the end their forwards became very dangerous. During extra time, however, when they played one short, following injury to a forward, Bishops Tawton gained the winning goal through Meadows.

The Cup was presented to the Bishops Tawton captain by the small daughter of the President of the competition (Rev. Walter Brown).

(Continued from Previous Column.)

of wild flowers (decorative)—J. Tarr, J. Stuckey, Chittlehamholt; May Yendell, North Molton.
JUVENILES
Posy of wild flowers—R. Yendell, North Molton; H. Elworthy, South Molton; V. Slade, Chulmleigh. Essay, "The town or village in which I live"—R. Yendell; D. Slade, Chulmleigh; M. Buckingham.

There was also a programme of field sports.

The Bishops Tawton team seem to have been particularly successful over the years.
N. DEVON JOURNAL.

Bishops Tawton Winners! The Captain, Albert Lock on the shoulders and Jack Nutt on the right. Thought to be in the 1940s.

115

This was taken in the mid '50s. Reg Shapland, Fred Ovey, Ernie Ovey, Eric Bennet, Bill McManus, Bill Brayley, Len Turner, Ernie Jago, Alfie Barrow and Charlie Hillson.

Left: *Pete Hooper, professional footballer and landlord.*

Peter Hooper, Landlord of the Three Pigeons for many years and a resident here for many more years was a professional footballer who played for Bristol Rovers, Bristol City and Cardiff. He ran a football team in the village, that played in the North Devon Sunday League.

Brian Ford

In 1952 Local businessman Brian Ford played football in Bishops Tawton for the reserve team. He went on to be a director of Plymouth Argyle in the mid 1970s. This was a particularly successful time for Plymouth which was highlighted by winning promotion in 1974/5 season.

Michael Beer tells us there was a very good Policeman called Fred Chapple who was very interested in the football team. After the Second World War there was a good team that came over from Russia called the Moscow Dynamos. Fred called our team the Bishops Tawton Dynamos after that! Every Saturday, when they were playing, he'd go over and raise the flag so you would know the Bishops Tawton Dynamos were playing at home!

Cricket

Cricket started long ago. The first definite documented mention of cricket was in 1598 at a court case in Guildford, Surrey. Gambling was a big part of cricket. The game thrived after 1660 and attracted gamblers making large bets. The 1664 Gaming Act limited stakes to £100 the equivalent of £13,000 in present day money. In the last half of the eighteenth century press reports focused on betting results

Some players are recognized here: Bill Slee, Leonard Avery, Edward Waldron, Michael Blackmore and Mr Ayres was the umpire.

rather than on the game itself. Now the emphasis is clearly on the standard of play. In the past gamblers formed their own teams to improve their chances of winning their bets. Many of the patrons were the nobility and they employed experts from village teams as the earliest professionals.

In Bishops Tawton cricket was a regular weekly village activity, not only for the players but many villagers too. They would spend their afternoon watching or helping with the teas. Cricket took place on the Marsh Field which is part of Court Farm, by the river bank. There was a small pavilion built on stilts to avoid damage from flooding.

James Waldron remembers, when he was a young-ster cricket was an important thing in the village. His father always played for the cricket team, as well as Bill Slee and Jack Nutt. He said it was all local people. They played all the local villages as far away as Lynton. He remembers going down to Lynton with the cricket club. The path to the cricket pitch needed doing up and the only way they could do it was to create a footpath so the County Council took over the path and took over responsibility for main-taining it.

Sadly, first the cricket team folded and then the

An early photograph of the cricket team.

pavilion was set on fire and vandalized.

Cyril Dennis remembers the cricket team too, *"Mr Slee the butcher was a really good cricketer, Jack Anderton, Tommy Down and Dennis Knight played too."*

Jean Ford remembers going to watch cricket as a child. She used to help Mrs Smalldon do the teas. There were home made cakes and sandwiches. Lots of villagers would go down and watch and some took deck chairs. She remembers sitting up on the river bank to watch.

117

Could this be the Pavilion in the background? Edward Waldron, Mr Birchall, Dougie Lock, Mr Ayres, Mr Stanbury, Bill Slee and Jack Nutt were part of this side.

The cricket team. Jim Symons, Roy Taylor, Dougie Lock, Albert Lock, Jack Nutt, Don Luckhurst, Lloyd Parker, Charlie Hilson, Tommy Donovan, Bob Mellows, Ted Turner, Bert Ensor.

Meg Runnalls remembers walking over to watch the cricket.

Janet Law remembers her father, Mr Kitt, was very involved in the cricket and he used to cut the grass. Janet used to help to keep the scores and her mum used to do the teas. She used to collect water from the butchers to make the tea. She remembers the butcher, Mr Slee being a very good bowler.

Patricia Andrews and Vicki White remember their father Bill Slee was a good cricketer. They always went to cricket on a Saturday in the summer. Their mother cooked cakes and did teas. It was really part of village life. Other players they remember were Jack Nutt, Edward Waldron, Jimmy Fogwell, Mr Avery, Jim Symons. Mr Ayre was the umpire for the team and Mr Kitt the secretary. If the tide was high the path would be covered, sometimes you had to climb over the railway line to reach the pitch.

Mr Slee, cricketer and butcher. NDJ ATHENAEUM COLLECTION ND RECORD OFFICE.

Right: *Jim Symons, Jack Nutt and Bill Slee, Austin Burridge, Harold Parkhouse, Brian Smalldon, Lenard Avery and Dennis Knight can be seen here.* NDJ ATHENAEUM COLLECTION ND RECORD OFFICE.

A game of cricket in progress on the marsh field with Codden Hill in the background. Jim Symons is the wicket keeper. NDJ ATHENAEUM COLLECTION ND RECORD OFFICE.

This picture shows the early days of the club in the Village Hall. Front row, Jennifer Goody, Christine Shapland, Anne West, ?, ?, Maureen Holland. Back row, ?, ?, Les Geen, Nigel Taylor, Bob Mellows, ?, ?, Brian Ford, Michael Beer ?, Tony Vickery and David Burgess.

Badminton

The game originated in India, it was particularly popular in the British garrison town of Poona (now Pune). The game was first called Poona. It was taken back to England by retired officers. It is thought that badminton was named after Badminton House, Gloucester, owned by the Duke of Beaufort. Back in 1893, the Badminton Association of England first published a set of rules for the game. Badminton was a demonstration event in the 1972 Summer Olympics and it became an official Olympic Sport in 1992.

The *North Devon Journal Herald* records that Bob Mellows founded The Badminton Club in Bishops Tawton in 1958. Lines were drawn on the floor of the Village Hall marking out the badminton court. The group in Bishops Tawton started with twenty members. They moved on to play in larger halls in Barnstaple and ended up in the Sports Hall at Park School. George Shapland was an active member and ran the junior section of the club. The club's membership at one time reached fifty-five and for a long time from the mid seventies they dominated competitive badminton in North Devon. The club celebrated twenty-five years and a special dinner was held for past and present members.

Chris Shapland remembers walking up the hill in the village with her friend and seeing Brian Ford cycling down the hill. He stopped and shouted across the road telling them that they were starting a badminton club and asking if they were interested. He asked them to a meeting back in 1958.

At one time the Ladies First Team was famous for being undefeated. After 13 January 1975 they won their next 85 matches.

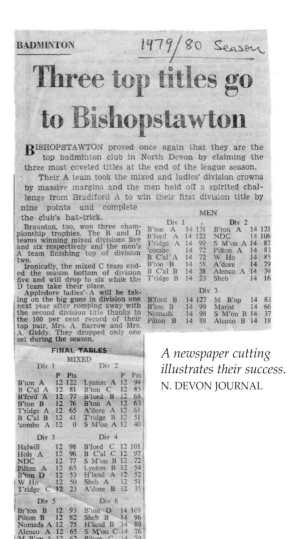

A newspaper cutting illustrates their success.
N. DEVON JOURNAL

Badminton players celebrating with the cups they won. Paul Shapland, Alan Schofield, Janet Conway, Graham Saunders, Janet Turner, Bob Mellows, David Burgess, Jill Skelton, George Shapland, Anne Marie Wisemen, Sarah Pitney, Paul Widecombe, Alison Down, Barbara Bidgood, Christine Shapland, Chris Skelton. Probably taken in 1980s.

Christine Shapland remembers the cold winter of 1963. They team had an away game at Combe Martin and Brian Ford drove. They squashed three in the front and three in the back. They got to the hill approaching Combe Martin and found it was impassable so they had to turn around and take another route. When they finally arrived they found the team had converted an old barn at the back of The Pack of Cards pub into a badminton court. There were stone floors and two old oil heaters.

Ice Skating

This seems an unlikely sport for a Devon village but several people remember the field behind the mill being flooded and icing over. Many residents used it for ice-skating.

Chapter 10

Bishops Tawton in Wartime

"I answer my country's call to do my bit you see Side by side with blokes who fight, out there for you and me
I am proud to answer her call, to help defend the free
For it's better to die in battle than to lose your liberty."

Extract from "My Country's Call", A wartime poem by Bert Verney of Overton.

World War One. 1914-1918

When war was declared in 1914, a large proportion of the men in the parish would have worked in some way in connection with agriculture. In addition to farm labour, many working men who were employed on the Hall estate enlisted, as was the case with so many more large country houses at that time. This depleted the local workforce significantly resulting in major changes in the way such large estates were managed. Although the farms retained some workers, the majority of those employed in the house or as gardeners were called up and large numbers of horses from farms were also requisitioned. The loss of life and changes in the way of country living meant that for everyone during and after the war, things would never quite be the same again.

In this centenary year of the outbreak of the First World War, research into the men with a connection to Bishops Tawton who lost their lives in WW1 is underway. A summary is given below. Much of this information has been researched by Brian Barrow, a local WW1 historian and Dianne Lyddon, a local family history researcher.

Private Walter John Balman. Second Battalion, Devonshire Regiment.
Died aged 26. 1918. Served with the Hampshire Regiment and formerly 3/1st Royal North Devon Hussars. Missing in action. Son of Walter and Florence Balman of Fordegate and husband of Daisy. Previously worked as a slaughterman. Commemorated at Comines-Warneton, Hainaut, Belgium.

Gunner William Beer.
Died aged 32. Royal Marine Artillery, HMS *Lion*. Son of Mary Beer, Elms Cottage. Before he enlisted, William had been a parcel clerk at Barnstaple Junction Station.

Private George Boughton.
Died aged 23. He was the only son of Frederick and Bessie Boughton. Frederick, his father, had been the arresting policeman involved in the case of the infamous John 'Babbacombe' Lee, "The man they couldn't hang".

Lt Col B. G. Davie of the 8th London Regiment. PO Rifles.
He lived at The Elms. He died as a result of illness contracted in service. His parents had a brass tablet mounted on oak erected in Bishops Tawton church to the memory of their son and 13 others who lost their lives. This was unveiled by the Bishop of Crediton .

Private H. S. Gollop
1917. Died in France.

Private Walter Goodenough
Died March 1915, fighting against the Turks. Son of Mr and Mrs Goodenough of Pullery Cottage, Bishops Tawton. The Goodenoughs also had three other sons in the Services.

Private A. S. Gregory.
Died age 21. 1915. Previously worked as a horseman at Chittlehampton.

Private William Harris.
Died aged 28. Signaller. Reported wounded and missing after the Battle of Loos in France. Son of W. Harris of Hall.

Leading Seaman Robert Holmes.
Died age 44. 1914. Lost to the disaster to HMS *Hawke* when it was torpedoed by a U-boat in the North Sea.

Gunner George Thomas Houle.
Died aged 24 in Tidworth Hospital. Son of John Houle of Fisherton Farm.

Private E. Parkhouse.

Sergeant William James Ridd.
Son of Mrs Ridd, licence holder of the Chichester Arms. Wounded in France. He was with his friend, Private S. Smith, also of Bishops Tawton, who was also wounded at the same time. Pte Smith survived.

Sapper Arthur Steer.

Died aged 32 in 1917. Royal Engineers. A carpenter who had been born in Bishops Tawton. Died in Kent from a spinal complaint after contracting measles.

Private Arthur Taylor.

Died aged 24. Son of George and Ellen Taylor of High Cross, Easter Street, Bishops Tawton. Served with his brother George who saw Arthur dying on the battlefield.

Private Robert Tolley.

Died aged 24. 1916. 2nd/6th Battalion of the Devonshire Regiment. Died in India of a fever. Previously a baker's servant. His father was the policeman in Bishops Tawton. No fewer than seven members of the Tolley family of served in the wars.

Private Ernest Westcott

Died age 27. Brother of Miss L. R. Westcott of "The Stores", Bishops Tawton.

Killed in action in France.

Private Stanley Wonnacott.

Aged 24. 1918 Missing in Flanders. Son of Thomas and Mary Wonnacott of High Bickington. Before the war Stanley had worked with one of his elder brothers Fred as a grocer. Fred continued to run the Bishops Tawton Stores until about 1930.

There are another 81 names recorded on the Bishops Tawton War Memorial of those who also served and had some connection to the parish. One was Private Jack Morrish, son of Mr and Mrs John Morrish, who was in the Devon and Dorset Regiment. He lied about his age to join early and served in France. He recounted a story of seeing two of his own men carrying a box of ammunition; it was hit by a shell, he saw the explosion and he saw nothing of either of his comrades again. Jack was treated for trench foot. He was also wounded twice on the same day but following treatment was able to resume duty. He returned home safely to work with his father and eventually run the family building business at Chestwood.

Mr John Tanton of East Street had served with the 2nd Devons for twelve years, five of those in India for which he received a medal (Burma Clasp). He latterly worked as a platelayer with the railway company. He died having lived in Bishops Tawton for forty-seven years in 1939 at the age of seventy-five years, survived by his widow and 16 children. At the time of his death he was recorded as being a Chelsea Pensioner.

There is also a grave in Bishops Tawton church-yard of Ernest Firth of Newport who was one of the lucky ones to have survived the First World War. He fought on the Somme in the trenches in relentless rain

Private Arthur Taylor of Easter Street, killed in action. Brother-in-Law of Jack Morrish.

John (known as Jack) Morrish sitting on the right. Taken during active service in WW1.

Ernest Firth. WW1 Soldier who survived the Somme trenches and is buried in Bishops Tawton churchyard.

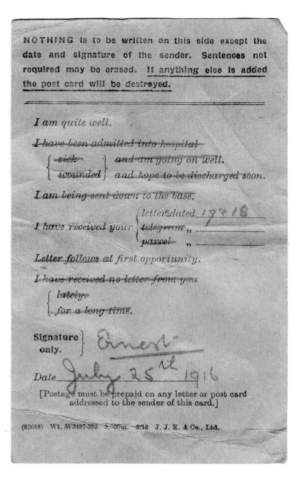

Card sent by Ernest Firth to his parents from the battlefield.

and mud. His personal diary, in the hands of his descendants today, reads "Heavy bombardment all night" and then the diary abruptly stops. His family say that he was buried alive in a trench on the Somme. Fortunately he was dug out and did eventually come back to England. He spent a lot of time in hospital and though he recovered from his injuries, the experience of war for him meant that his health was never quite the same again.

A number of the Lock and Isaac brothers from Bishops Tawton served in this war. In December 1915 the fathers of the boys both received letters from His Majesty the King congratulating them on each having four serving sons. The sons of Mr Isaac were Herbert in Kitchener's Army, Ernest in the Australian contingent, Sidney in the Royal Marines and Cecil serving in India. None are recorded as having lost their lives in the war. Thomas Lock, who lived at that time in Town Tenement, had twelve children with the following four sons all serving in WW1: William with the North Devon Hussars, Frederick in India, Percy in Exmouth and Harold in Northumberland. All survived but Harold Lock is sadly reported as later losing his life in World War Two.

Probably as a consequence of there being no large

parish hall at the time, an entry in the Bishops Tawton School (now the Village Hall) Log Book in 1915 stated
"The school was closed for a morning in consequence of a detachment of the Devon Regiment visiting the village when the school was required for serving them with refreshments."

Nothing was wasted in wartime, everything had a use and everyone helped with the war effort in some way. Another entry from the Bishops Tawton School Log Book made on 3 September 1918 states
"The children were asked to bring plum stones and nut shells to school as they are required by the ministry of munitions."

These were apparently collected across the country and in the USA at that time to extract carbon for use in gas masks needed to protect soldiers from chlorine gas attacks.

Another entry at that time records that the older scholars in the charge of their teachers, went out gathering blackberries for the purpose of national jam making: "25 pounds were sent to Barnstaple."

Captain and Mrs Davie from the Elms who had lost a son in the war, are recorded as having sent a

Looking down towards the Bushens from Bishops Tawton churchyard in the early 1920s. In this picture, the War Memorial has been newly erected giving the names of those who served and those who had lost their lives in WW1. The main road through the village had not been widened at this time.

The same view in 2014, in the centenary year of the First World War. Another plaque had been added to the base of the memorial after the Second World War to record another six names.

number of items to the Barnstaple War Supply Depot. These depots were found in most towns and were run by private individuals to supply items for frontline war hospitals for injured soldiers. Items would have been made by volunteers with donated materials, often to Red Cross patterns. The following were recorded as sent by the Davie family on this occasion: 13 mufflers (thick scarves), 11 pairs of socks, 12 pairs of mittens, 2 flannel shirts, 2 bed jackets and 1 helpless case jacket (this being a garment designed to be used without unduly moving a severely injured patient).

The imposing War Memorial in Bishops Tawton churchyard was erected to commemorate the men from the parish who lost their lives in the 1914-1918 Great War. It was erected and dedicated in 1919.

Those who returned came back to a changed world. Life on farms was changing and new opportunities for work were offered. In Bishops Tawton, as across the country, there was work to be found locally in connection with building: New roads, new bridges, new housing and improvements to existing houses. Newbridge was built and opened over the Taw, the main road through Bishops Tawton was widened with a new section added near Court Farm. Many new houses were built in the village in the 1920s and '30s, the years between the wars.

World War Two. 1939-1945

When war was declared again in 1939, a large number of local men volunteered or were conscripted to join the services.

There are six men from Bishops Tawton recorded as having lost their lives in WW2:

Sub/Lt Norris Vaux Heppenstall.
1945. Royal Naval Volunteer Reserve. Served on HMS *Indefatigable*.
Son of Philip and Florence Heppenstall.

Sergeant Harold J. Lock.
Son of Thomas and Laura Lock of Town Tenement. Buried in Yorkshire.
Two other brothers of Harold, Albert and Douglas also served in WW2 war but returned safely to Bishops Tawton.

Gunner W. H. Newcombe.
Of Overton Cottages. Died as a result of war service. Buried in Bishops Tawton.

Private Robert J. Smalldon.
Age 39. 1945. Army Catering Corp. Attached to Royal Corp of Signals.
Son of Robert and Ellen Smalldon. War Grave: Antwerp, Belgium.

Corporal Francis Tolley.
Age 23. 1943. Royal Corps of Signals. Son of Francis and Annie Tolley of Easter (now East) Street. War Grave: Kanchanaburi – the main Prisoner of War cemetery in Thailand for victims of the building of the Burma railway.

Flight Officer Stanley John Verney.
1943. 218 Sqdn. Royal Air Force Volunteer Reserve. Of Overton Farm.
War Grave: Hanover, Germany.

Some other local people have their own and family wartime stories:

Bob Mellows lived with his family in South View in Chestwood. As a young man he joined the local Air Training Corp. (ATC) and later, fired up by stories of well known heroes such as Douglas Bader, both he and his brother joined the RAF. Bob volunteered as air crew. He travelled to Canada to do his training in Newfoundland as the facilities were there and it was safer than England. He subsequently flew as a bomb aimer, recalling how the pilots would pick their crew and how they all looked at the notice boards each morning to see which sections would be flying. They then had to plot their own maps, following dog leg routes to avoid German radar. On some missions they would be flying for as long as eleven hours.

Bob Mellows, RAF. Later to become the well known Bishops Tawton newsagent.

Bob Mellows on the left with aircrew. 1944.

Bob said he gave little thought to the danger of flying on bombing raids but the reality at the time was that you were lucky to survive five trips. On average, two out of five would not make it. He says they never discussed the casualty rate between them, just got on with the job. Bob remembers being given a set bombing time and they had to calculate the journey to be able to make it spot on, even allowing for variable weather conditions. On three occasions, they had to make "Manna runs" to Holland to alleviate starvation. The Germans had cut off the food supply chains and the RAF had agreed to help. Bob says they had to fly dangerously low to drop food parcels, to which they had added their own sweet rations.

After the war Bob found it difficult to return to his previous job. What he really wanted to do was to be a sports trainer. He started a very successful badminton club in Bishops Tawton and also started his own business, running the village newsagents

Albert Ensor, father of Grace Elliott who lived in Fair View, had served in the regular Army for twelve years, including a posting to India. He caught malaria which affected his long term health. He had to stop playing with the Bishops Tawton football team because of the after effects. The malaria left him with fevers which made him shiver and sweat. Grace

Roy Taylor of Bishops Tawton on the right when he was serving in Malta in 1941.

127

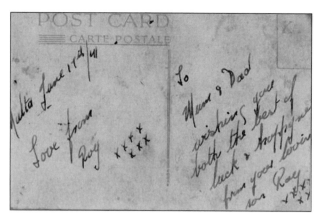

Reverse of the picture postcard sent by Roy Taylor to his parents William and Maria Taylor of Newbridge House.

Albert Lock when stationed in London.

can remember her mother always having to light fires in the bedroom fireplace for him and that he used to wrap up in old army heavy great coat to try and warm up when he had fevers.

Three of the Lock brothers served in WW2. In addition to Harold Lock who had served in the First World War but lost his life in the second, his brother Albert Lock had been posted to the guns defending London stationed in Barking, Essex. His daughter Jean recalls the family story that he was such a good marksman at home shooting rabbits that it was a natural progression for him to have such a posting. Their brother Douglas also served in France and was evacuated from the Dunkirk beaches as part of Operation Dynamo in 1940. He spoke very little about his wartime experiences but did tell his family that to avoid being shot on the beaches they had to wade out into the sea up to their necks and wait to be picked up by boat. Following his safe return, Douglas resumed his work with the Morrish family builders in the village, eventually taking over the business.

Sergeant Douglas Lock (fifth from left, back row) when serving in WW2. He was evacuated from Dunkirk.

The War for the Verney Brothers

The late Bert Verney, who lived with his family at Overton Farm, recalls in his autobiography how, in 1941, both he and his brother Stanley had wanted to volunteer to join the RAF. Both felt strongly about it but being needed to work on the farm, only one could go and Bert explained how the whole future was eventually decided between them that day on the single spin of a coin. Stanley, the elder of the two joined up and Bert stayed home to work on the farm with his father.

Bert and Stanley Verney with their sister Claire.

In 1941 Bert, who had been in the Local Defence Volunteers, was asked to join a secret and special branch of the Home Guard. This was one of four in North Devon described as an underground movement with secret bases in woods, mines and quarries. The local branch Bert joined was hidden in Tawstock woods. This group, designed to be a stronger line of defence in the event of an invasion, was well armed and trained in combat and in the use of explosives and booby traps. He recalls how they were trained by undertaking "attacks" at Chivenor, a gun emplacement at Instow and Barnstaple Railway Station.

The secret base in Tawstock woods was built into a hollow, covered with bushes, trees, earth and moss, with a safety chamber and an escape tunnel at the back. It was well stocked with ammunition, food and water.

Stanley Verney joined the RAF in 1941 and became a navigator and bomb aimer. He completed his training in America and Canada before being deployed on bombing raids to Germany. In 1943 he was reported as missing in action. His family say he tragically lost his life on what was to have been his last ever bombing raid.

Following the sad loss of his brother, Bert had held a dream to commemorate him by providing a playing field for the children of Bishops Tawton. This would not only be in memory of his brother, but for all those

from the parish of Bishops Tawton who lost their lives in the Second World War. The Verney family owned a field in the village and money was raised to undertake work on this to level it for a playing pitch and to equip it as a playground for children. It was the field which many had remembered as being "Maggy's field" – the horse which had pulled the Waldron farm milk cart. In the early 1970s, about thirty years after the loss of his brother, this became the Stanley Verney Playing Field. It was ceremoniously opened by Mr Charles Chichester of Hall and the day made into quite a village event with a fête held in the field.

Plaque on the entrance pillar to the Stanley Verney Playing Field commemorating the six men from the parish who failed to return from WW2.

Charles Chichester unveiling the plaque on the opening of the playing field. Early 1970s. From front left: Bert Verney, John Verney, Albert Verney (Stanley's father), Charles Chichester, Mrs Chichester, May Verney.

Stanley's sister, Claire, also organised a tribute to her brother by instigating the placement of a stone memorial bench at the top of Codden Hill. Many people will have used this, pausing and sitting to admire the wonderful view – looking out over the formerly Verney family farm of Overton towards Barnstaple and the North Devon coast in the distance.

The fête held in the new playing field on opening day. From left: Unknown, Charles Chichester, Mrs Chichester. Behind the stall are the Verney family: May, Diana, Claire, Albert, John and Bert.

The playing field today.

The Verney Memorial Bench on Codden Hill.

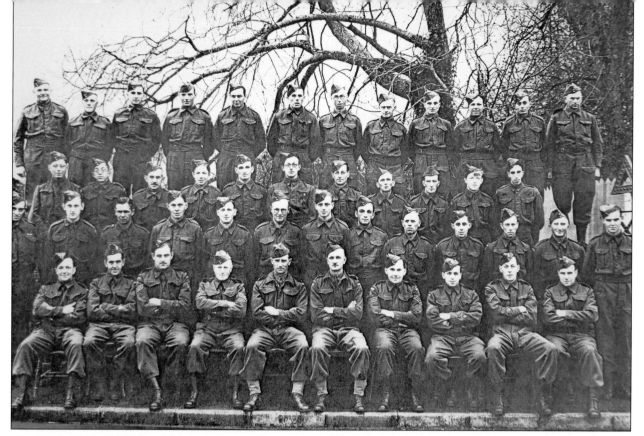

Home Guard. No.3 Platoon 'B' Company. Bishops Tawton. The year is not known. Back row from left: Harry Tossell, Arthur Hobbs, Jack Hill, Wilf Thomas, George Murch, Barney Hutchings, Stan Thomas, Bill Shapland, Wilf Turner, Harry Ford. Ernie Dodd, Unknown. Next row: Harry Andrews, Edward Lewis, Sid Moore, Ken Letheby, Charlie Scott, Ern Beer, Don Moody, Daniel Smalldon, Ernie Phillips, Prouse, Unknown. Next row: Jack Facey, Les Smalldon, Bill Hill, Sid Symons, Ern Dummet, George Huxtable, Pat Smalldon, Percy Ley, Walter Cook, Curly Hurst, Bill Dymond, Charlie Facey, Sid Squires. Front row: L/CPL Taffy Letheby, CPL Reg Barrett, SGT Ken Wythe, SGT Bert Harris, 2ndLT Jim Fogwell, LT Bill Slee, SGT Bill Harris, CPL Reg White, CPL Jim Symons, L/CPL Charles Trevisick.

Life on the Home Front

"Dads Army" – Bishops Tawton Home Guard

Originally known as the Local Defence Volunteers and later known as the Home Guard, this comprised men who were needed at home in reserved occupations such as farming, had medical reasons for not being signed up, were younger than eighteen, the conscription age, or who were older. Some of these older men would have served in WW1. The Bishops Tawton Platoon included men from the parish and surrounding area.

Bill Slee, who was also the local village butcher, led the Platoon and the training. His daughters, Patricia and Vicky, remember the Home Guard meeting for Sunday morning drill practice in their father's orchard which was behind the Bushens. Bert Verney had joined the Home Guard. He recalled how they started off meeting at the bottom of Codden Hill and armed themselves with anything they could find: hooks, air guns, long handled forks, poles with knives on the end and shotguns. They were later issued with uniforms, and a few proper rifles.

Bishops Tawton men also formed part of a local Royal Observer Corps in wartime. These were civilian volunteers, trained by professional officers in

Another picture of the Home Guard.

aircraft recognition, tracking and reporting of aircraft over Britain. Observers out in the field would track the position, height and movement of any aircraft and report this continually back to the command centre. At the centre, information would be marked on a large map on the plotting table. This information was crucial to warn and prepare for bombing raids.

*Bishops Tawton men in the Royal Observer Corp: 1940-
1941. Back row from left: Jack Morrish, Ponto Gibbons,
Arthur King, Harry Ayres, Dick Barrow, John Beer, Bill
Howard, Arthur Watts, Harry Hartnoll. Front row: Mr
Boatfield, Philip Oram, Mr Incledon, Unknown Officer,
John Kingdon, Bert Sexon, Jim Handford.*

Life was not the same for anyone at home. Grace
Elliott recalls that her father Albert was away for
years in the regular Army and her mother, as well as
looking after the family, had to go to work in
Brimley's munitions factory in Barnstaple. A lot of
the older men, like Grace's grandfather still had to go
and get work on farms, replacing the labour of the
younger men who were away at war. Grace remembers her grandmother also having to go out to work
doing washing to help with the family finances.

For those at home, changes in every day life had to
be made. Food was rationed and although this eased
slightly after the war, rationing did not completely
stop until 1954. Everyone who could, grew some of
their own food in a garden or allotment. During the
war years there were plenty of well cultivated allotments in Bishops Tawton. These were found below
the Gospel Hall and in the lower fields where Mount
Pleasant was later built. Descendants of many families in the parish also recall the keeping of chickens,
ducks or geese and a pig to fatten. They may either
have had their own pig, or shared the feeding of it –
and the eventual eating of it, with family or neighbours. This was supplemented by food which could
be caught and sold or eaten such as rabbits and elvers.

During the war, farmers were all given directives
by the Ministry of Food to grow extra crops to help
feed the nation. They were told what and how much
to grow. Much of the Codden Hill area was ploughed
to grow cereal crops and quite a large proportion was
given to growing potatoes.

Extra help was needed to help with the increased
work on the farms and whole families helped out at
harvest time. Cyril Dennis can recall as an eight-year-
old having to work with his father on Codden Hill in
the war years picking up potatoes. Bob Barrow
remembers Land Army girls at Woolstone who were
"always singing and larking about" but they worked
hard and got on with the job. They also had, at different times, both Italian and German prisoners of war
sent to help out on the farm. He can remember that
the German POWs were particularly hard working,
were treated well and allowed to come in and eat
their lunch in the farmhouse kitchen. One of them
made his aunt a pair of slippers out of string.

In support of the war effort, Bob can also recall
that behind Herner School there was a garden.
During the war the children would dig the garden to
produce leeks, cabbages and potatoes. He remembers that all the school children went out and picked
hips and haws from the hedgerows. These were sent
to Bristol in the train and used to make medicine –
Rosehip Syrup which was a valuable source of vita-
mins. This carried on until the 1950s. The school
would be sent the money for funds, some of which
would be used to buy the children presents at
Christmas.

In 1944, Bishops Tawton School took part in the
national "Salute the Soldier" campaign. The Head
teacher recorded in the School Log Book at the time
that the school had received a certificate of honour for
reaching its target. This was an extension of the
National Savings Campaign specifically for the war
effort. It was undertaken during Salute the Soldier
week which included marches and other pageantry
across the country supporting different branches of
the armed forces.

Jean Shapland remembers being sent by her
mother to get things from Ford and Lock's shop. She
recalls she would take the ration book and queue up.
She says she was always told by her mother that she
was to start by saying, "would you oblige mother by
… " then asking for what was needed. About two
ounces cut from great lumps of butter or cheese were
all they could have on rations.

People did help each other out a lot during the
war. Bob Barrow recalls that he went to the wedding
of Dora Gollop, the assistant school mistress at
Herner, who got married to Stan Thomas, a relation
of his. Afterwards, in the Parish Church Rooms, he
remembers having the unusual luxury at that time of
some wedding cake made with dried fruit.
Ingredients for making that cake had been collected
by people from around the village – the sultanas and
currants, small amounts all donated from individual's rations to help make a nice cake. He remembers
that Dora took some to the school on the following
Monday morning for the other children to taste.

Evacuees

Many families with spare rooms in the parish were asked to take in evacuees during the WW2. Michael Beer has memories of the evacuee children arriving in the village, being in the Village Hall and being allocated to families within the parish. He remembers living in Sunnyside on New Road at the time and his family had to take in three evacuees, two girls and a boy. For many local families, this was the first time they had met anyone from a city, being quite unaware of what it was like to be bombed. Most of the children evacuated had never been to the country before, never seen farm animals and told stories of playing on bomb sites. It was not always easy adjusting on both sides but it was a necessary contribution to the war effort. Many children made new friendships which endured. Some local evacuees, like Mavis Courtenay, returned to the village when they grew up. Mavis married Gerald Courtenay, and ran the Bishops Tawton Post Office for many years.

The picture below was taken in front of the gates to the Vicarage in about 1941. It is recalled both as a celebration of the 100th anniversary of the building of the Church School and as a picture of all the school along with evacuee children who were welcomed during the war to the parish. Some of the older children who had already left school are in the picture and came back for the occasion. Certainly the number of children here is greater than the normal school roll at the time and evacuee children are included in this picture.

Some of those identified are: Brian Ford in the centre, he has a bandage on his head from an operation. Michael Beer is in front of him. The Headmistress was Miss Coleman, on the right. Also on the right are the Methodist minister and his wife,

Mr and Mrs Bird. At the other end was the vicar and his wife, Mr and Mrs Nicholas. Some other children included in this picture are: Bill Oram, Jack Anderton, Margaret and Raymond Skinner, Shirley and Robert Rogers, Gordon Cook, Pam and Graham Burridge and Frank Harris.

A report from the *North Devon Journal* at the time stated:

> *"The Villagers of Bishops Tawton, have from the first, displayed a great and friendly interest in their evacuee guests. Their great gesture has been the organisation of a large scale entertainment of the whole of the evacuated children. The party was arranged by the Bishops Tawton Social Welfare Committee (Chairman Mr Thomas) which is representative of the village community."*

Bob Barrow, who had lived at Fisherton for a short while, had moved with his family to Kent. When the war started, the family had a very close encounter with a crashed German aircraft. It had come down in a field near them and the family went to have a look. Bob distinctly remembers two Germans standing in the road and one of them saying to the Home Guard " You will treat me correctly as we will be here in two weeks." This made his parents decide immediately to send him back to Bishops Tawton as an evacuee to his uncle at Woolstone Farm. He remembers his mother putting him on the train at Waterloo, and that he travelled alone, standing for six hours on the packed train all the way from London to Barnstaple. He then got to Bishops Tawton on the carrier seat of his uncle's bike. He had to work hard and help with all the jobs on the farm. For many years after moving back to London he would save his pocket money to be able to come back to Bishops Tawton and work on the farm in his holidays. After completing his

Bishops Tawton school children and evacuees 1941.

Bob Barrow as a boy when an evacuee at Herner School.

Bob in later years. NORTH DEVON JOURNAL.

National Service, Bob eventually came back to Barnstaple to live in the 1950s.

There are other memories of life in wartime Bishops Tawton.

Janet Law recalls how in the years of the Second World War, her father (Mr Kitt) used to organise concerts in the Village Hall in aid of "the local lads" – local boys who were away in the Army. He got various people involved in these – doing all sorts of things. Janet remembers that he had a type of puppet he performed with. She was seven or eight years old at the time and learning ballet so he got her to dance at the concerts.

Most people, who had a spare room in the war years, if they did not have evacuees staying, would rent out their rooms. Jean Ford remembers lots of people in the village had lodgers; every room in the house was used.

Andy Bament recounts a story that his mother told him. She said that the hayrick at Cross Farm was "the best guarded hayrick of the war". This apparently being due to the fact that the policeman, who should have been out checking hayricks in the parish – to make sure German sympathisers were not setting fire to them to guide enemy planes – spent a considerable amount of his time drinking tea in the farm kitchen!

Roy and Jean Shapland, née Dennis, can remember the Americans frequently passing through Bishops Tawton in Army lorries on their way to Chivenor, Woolacombe and Saunton. As children they would wait with their friends for the lorries to go by and shout "any gum chum" and would often get lucky.

There was a Mr Ridd who lived at Hills View who had been a prisoner of war for some years. At that time his wife is remembered as taking in holiday guests. She also kept an allotment in the land opposite her house below the Gospel Hall and is remembered locally as being very generous with produce and generally helpful to others despite her situation and the needs of her own family. Thankfully her husband returned safely to great celebration in the village.

Michael Beer can remember that during the war years there was a man from the Ministry of Information called Mr Hutton who went around the parishes showing cine film on what would happen if there was an invasion and what we would be expected to do. He also showed films for children on Saturday mornings in the Church Rooms, what we now call the Village Hall. At the time he lived in the village Reading Room for a while.

As the war progressed there were opportunities to get materials needed for building. Cyril Dennis remembers that lorries would arrive full of reclaimed building materials from the war. Hussey's he thinks they were called. They were full of materials reclaimed from bomb sites that people could buy.

Elvie Snow can remember that after the war an outdoor party was held to celebrate. This took place under the chestnut trees in the centre of the village; she remembers that they dragged a piano out of someone's house.

Chapter 11

Bishops Tawton School

"The pool was eventually constructed but it was difficult to try and learn to swim as it was so cold, even in summer."

Sue Squire

The plaque below can be found on the Village Hall. It tells us that there was a National School here in 1841. A little bit of history explains what was happening.

Plaque on the Village Hall.

National Schools were founded in the nineteenth century by the National Society for Promoting Religious Education. They provided elementary education in accordance with the teaching of the Church of England to the children of the poor. Before this time education for the poorer families was limited to some Charity Schools and Sunday Schools.

The Education Act of 1870 set up Board Schools; they abolished school fees, extended the curriculum and introduced compulsory attendance.

The 1902 Education Act put the main part of elementary education in the hands of the Local Education Authority. Board Schools became Council Schools and Voluntary Schools and were funded from the rates.

The 1944 Education Act replaced Voluntary Schools with Controlled and Aided Schools and Council Schools became known as County Primary Schools.

A quote from the local newspaper tells us that there was a smaller school before this.

North Devon Journal Herald
10 June 1841
"Bishops Tawton:- The interesting ceremony of

laying the foundation stone of the new school room in this populous parish was performed in the afternoon of yesterday (Wednesday). The site selected for the building is the corner of the churchyard, just opposite the handsome and commodious vicarage house now in progress. The want of a school room of adequate dimensions has been long felt: for although by the liberality of the Duke of Bedford, the lower apartments of the Court-house have been appropriated to the purpose of the school, yet the increasing number of children has demanded larger accommodation. Mrs Baker laid the stone. We learnt that the dimensions of the school will be 41 feet by 24; the work is contracted for by Messrs Davy and sons of this town, who are building the parsonage house."

So groups of children were educated in the Old School building, which is the present Village Hall, from 1841 to 1932.

What did the children who were educated in the old Village School look like?

A damaged picture, but it shows a very early group of children outside the school.

Bishops Tawton school children around 1905. The teacher is Miss Ethel Sexon. Top row left to right, Jimmy Hodge, Harry Tossel, Wilfred Webber, Jack Gabriel, Arthur Vaddon, Mabel Taylor, Harry Gabriel, Annie Pierce, Phylis Prideaux, Lottie Beer, Daisy Fogwell, Blanch Wills, Gertie Hammet, Louise Slee, Reggie Slee, Minnie Slee, Elsie Harper, Gertie Murch, D. Taylor, Lily Fogwell, Rosie Fogwell, Evelyn Cudmore, Edith Hammet, Billy Hill, John Beer, Evan Bowen, George Bowen, Jack Shaddick and Archie Skimmer.

Another group outside the old school. There are only a couple of children named here, Doreen Lock and Edna Laura Lock.

Bishops Tawton School in the present Village Hall. Some children are named as Daisy Taylor, Winnie Isaac, Mabel Tanton, Gladys Tucker, Lily Ridd, Edna Hill, Lily Tanton, Lucy Parsons.

This shows a teacher, Mr Dick Taylor with his pupils. He was the first one to live in the School House. This house is opposite the Almshouses in Bishops Tawton today.

This picture shows the school children outside the school in the present Village Hall. It is dated around 1930. Olive Brown (Née Morrish) is in the middle row fourth from the left.

The previous photographs show some of the children but what was it like to be a child at Bishops Tawton School in those early days?

Headteachers wrote several entries a week in the School Log Book as a diary of events within the school. They are only available up to the early '50s for public access at the North Devon Record Office. In a quote from the School Log Book in the HMI Examination Report of December 1896 we get a flavour of the curriculum that the children endured!

"The discipline is deserving of praise. A beginning has been made with musical drill and singing by note has been successfully taken. The needlework exercises were good, but in patching the selvedge of the patch should run in the same direction as that of the material. The premises have been much improved and are now very nice."

In March 1898, *"Today the first class boys have begun the map of Ireland, drawing it on their slates."*

Times were very different for children.

The Log Book of October 1897,
"I reported the non attendance of Charles Pike whom the Attendance Officer said had gone to work for a person in Barnstaple. He is twelve years of age and has not even tried to get a labour certificate."

The 1908 Inspectors' report declares "The provision of a playground would be a great advantage."

Ronald Down went to school in the Old School building in the early 1920s. He recalls ringing the bell five minutes before school started to give children time to get there because he said not everyone had a clock in their houses. He remembered going home for lunch. He said there were three classes, the big room was split into two classes and the third class was in the smaller room. He remembered his school days with fondness.

It also gives us insight into what life was like in the village at that time.

In 1908 the Log Book records:
"I have again warned the children about rushing from the school premises when they are dismissed, into the roads, as motor cars are often passing at a rapid rate down the hill."

It is thought that Captain Archibald Campbell who reputedly lived at Kings Cottage was the first owner of the horseless carriage in the whole of Devon. Villagers often had to help him get his car to the top of the hill through the village. This was around 1905.

This is Captain Campbell in a later model.
N. DEVON RECORD OFFICE.

In 1909 the Log Book quotes,
"I warned the boys today against throwing their hats at cyclists passing the school. Two boys had been guilty of this offence during playtime."

There are many entries about poor health; measles, whooping cough, influenza and it is noted diphtheria even caused the whole school to be closed for long periods. There were holidays granted for many local and national events from royal occasions to the need for farming labour.

Local events such as the fair and the circus in town often meant an extra half day holiday. There were many days of holiday given for celebrations related to the monarch at the time.

For example, in 1923,
"The school was closed today the children being granted a holiday at the request of the King, it being the wedding day of the Duke of York."

Other entries refer to the First World War and we gain glimpses into the ways the village children were involved. There is more information on this in the Wartime chapter.

There were public examinations. At that time secondary education was divided and to progress to Barnstaple Grammar School children took an entrance exam.

The Log Book of 1920 tells us,
"Two boys, John Challis and Fred Smalldon passed the examination qualifying them for a free place at Barnstaple Grammar School."

In 1925,
"Susan Chapman gained a free place at the Grammar School and will proceed there at the beginning of next term."

So girls too were successful from the education delivered at the Old School building.

This picture illustrates the seriousness of school at the time. Classrooms today are so brightly decorated and welcoming. Prize giving at Bishops Tawton School in 1954. FROM THE ATHENAEUM COLLECTION, NDJ.

A New School

In November 1930 the plans of the new school were on view. It was built by the Western Builder, F. W. Drake also by Morrish and Pickard.

The new school was opened in January 1932 with due ceremony.

So what was life like for the children in the new school? How did things change?

Again the School Log book offers some glimpses into the school day and memories of some village people illustrate their experiences.

School Log Book. FROM THE ATHENAEUM COLLECTION.

Remember the Milk?

The 1944 Education Act decreed that the Local Education Authority should provide milk, meals and other refreshments for pupils in attendance at schools maintained by the Authority. They had realised that hungry children could not learn. War was the spur to raise the standard of the nation's health and helped to maintain morale. At this time the children at Bishops Tawton were given small bottles of milk to drink each day. There were no fridges to keep them cool so they were either warm or frozen depending on the temperature outside on the day.

James Waldron recalls,
"We used to have the milk bottles, third of a pint bottles in those days delivered. Everybody had a third of a pint. I think I could earn three pence a week if I washed out the bottles and gathered them up."

Sue Squire remembers the time when the milk was frozen in the bottles and they had to drink it by breaking the ice with their straws.

Electricity at Last!

It wasn't until 1949 that the school had electricity. It is likely that gas lamps would have been used on those dark winter afternoons.

School re-opened to-day with a good a[t] and the addition of three new scholars Parsons has returned to duties and Mrs. is on Temporary duty also. She is a gre[at] to us.

During the past holiday fittings for th[e] light have been installed, but the su[pply] current is not yet laid [on]

A section of the School Log Book. A day in 1949 when electricity was installed, we are left wondering how long it took for the supply to be connected!

Playground Equipment and Exercise

On 1 July 1949 a new triple horizontal bar was fixed in the playground. It cost £13.13s.0d. and it cost £4.15s.0d. to fix it. The cost was covered by the Penny Bank fund set up in the old school.

Bishops Tawton children were renowned for gymnastic success. They had a film made about them with their teacher Mrs Cheetham to show other teachers how gymnastics should be taught. The children often did demonstrations in local fêtes and other events.

Denise Webber remembers her worst experience at school,

> "It was the climbing equipment on the bank, Lorna Holland (née Hutchings) was playing on it but she wouldn't let go, I took her hand off to help her, and she fell and broke her arm."

This shows Michael Blackmore, Christine Shapland, Kathleen Hind and Michael Gollop enjoying the playground equipment at Bishops Tawton school around 1950.

Below left: *This was taken in 1947. It shows Carol Cox, Michael Blackmore, Nigel Taylor and Jean Dennis.*
Below right: *Gymnastics became important. Here is Nigel Taylor practising his gymnastics.*

In 1948 there was a demonstration of gymnastics by the children for a WI fête at Tawton House.

Playground drill exercises.

Heating

Lorna Holland remembers

"My mum went to school which was in the Village Hall then and her family too. I went to this school. We had coal fires then and I always remember the little inkwells, brass inkwells. My mum was the caretaker and she had to clean these little inkwells every weekend. All the door handles were brass too and they had to be cleaned, I used to help her. She used to do the fires and keep them stoked up all day.

There is a shed on the side in school now where the coal used to be. She used to have to fill buckets and carry them to each fire. There were three fires."

Radio

The radio was used quite frequently for teaching a variety of subjects in school. Here it was used to mark the historical moment when Elizabeth was proclaimed Queen.

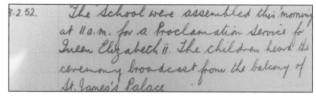

The School Log Book records the Proclamation Ceremony in 1952.

Uniform

A uniform at last! Blazer? Tie? Beret? Cap? What happened to them? Maybe you remember them. Still the same maroon colour is used today on school jumpers at Bishops Tawton School.

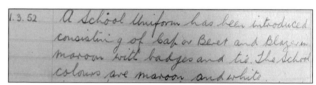

The School Log Book records the first uniform in 1952.

Christmas Parties and Concerts

There were parties and celebrations for Christmas, Mr Chichester from Hall is recorded as having supplied the Christmas tree, and every child received a present from under the tree. The parents provided teas and these were prepared by Mrs Holland, Mrs Beer and Mrs Dennis.

In June 1944 the school choir took part in an open air entertainment in the Vicarage grounds. There was maypole dancing, a play and choral speaking.

In December 1942 there was a Christmas concert given by the children at Bishops Tawton School. It lasted about three and a half hours! There were songs, solos and duets, choral speaking, plays, a pantomime in costume, country dancing, and items by the school percussion band. The proceeds came to over £15 and were presented to the Lord Mayor's Red Cross appeal and to the Prisoner of War Fund and a fund for a school piano was started.

Sports Days

There were sports days. The school was divided into houses for sport.

Grace Elliot remembers being in the Taw team. The sports were held on the cricket field that was part of Court Farm, next to the River Taw, instead of the school field as they are today. Jean and Roy Shapland remember the sack races and the slippery pole.

The School Log book dated 1 July 1953, records the sports were held on the Bishops Tawton cricket field, (the Marsh Field at Court Farm). Taw House won that year. Mr Chichester presented the cup to the winning house captains, Michael Croft and Jennifer Smart.

In 1959 The Rev. Alexander presented the cup to the captain of Manor House, the winning team. The individual prize winners that year were Colin Runnalls and Marjorie Nutt.

In 1960 the Inter Schools Sports were held in Bishops Tawton on the Marsh Field. Seven schools competed. Bishops Tawton won the Handicap Cup and the cup for the most points scored. The canteen staff were busy that day serving refreshments and teas on the field and the Bishops Tawton WI served teas in the Church Hall afterwards

Preparations for a Christmas Concert in 1944, Gordon Cook, Raymond Skinner, Jack Cox and Margaret Smalldon are here.

Christmas Concert 1960. A few children are named here. Linda Lock, Norman Facey, Wendy Heal, Dawn Tucker and Evelyn Biggs.

Sports Day at Bishops Tawton School on the marsh field in 1955. PICTURE FROM THE NDJ ATHENAEUM COLLECTION ND RECORD OFFICE.

Trips

There were school trips. Some people remember outings to the Gaumont Cinema in Barnstaple.

The School Log Book records on 3 March 1954 fifty two children were taken to see the film, 'The Conquest of Everest'. It was shown at the Gaumont Cinema.

Jean Shapland remembers lots of nature walks, going up through Hammets Lane towards Chestwood. They used to pick wild flowers and learn their names.

Testing

There were exams! At that time the year six tests were used to decide which form of secondary education you were most suitable to follow.

James Waldron remembered

"If you passed the eleven plus you went to the Grammar School and if you didn't you went to the Secondary Modern."

Michael Beer remembers,

"There were two parts to the test. Part 1 was taken here at Bishops Tawton School and Parson Nicholas

These girls were awarded a scholarship in passing the 11 plus exam in 1949. One of them tells us that there were only two boys in the year and neither of them passed. Elvie Snow, Cynthia Dummett, Muriel Allen, Margaret Johnson, Marjorie Newsham and Kathleen Hine.

oversaw that. The other part was at Barnstaple Grammar School (The Park School now). They had lunch at the Grammar School. I remember Sylvia Smalldon ran down the roads to tell me we had both passed the test."

A section from the School Log Book July 1946 the Headteacher records that he received news that nine of the twelve children who sat the scholarship exam to Barnstaple Grammar School had passed successfully. They were Robert Cox, G. Cook, Raymond Skinner, Michael Beer, Brian Ford, Sylvia Smalldon, Dorris Smalldon, Shirley Rogers, and Pamela Letheby. They all started at the Grammar School in September 1946. It also mentions Bernard Fisher who took the Metropolitan Exam and passed successfully. Even the youngest children were tested. The Log Book 16 Feb 1950 tells us that,

"All the children aged 6 years 9 months to 7 years 8 months took their age appropriate mental intelligence test today."

Maypole Dancing

Jean Ford remembered the maypole dancing at school. The boys had to carry the maypole out and put it up in the playground. Parents came to watch. They opened the window in the Headmaster's room and he had a gramophone for their dance music.

This was taken in 1948. Michael Gollop, Michael Blackmore, Terry Jones, Christine Shapland, Pat Eastman, Jean Ridd, Ian Taylor, Jean Shapland, Miss Coleman, Anne Willoughby and Margaret Burley are shown outside the present staffroom.

Percussion

Bishops Tawton children were very good at percussion and won prizes for it competing with other schools.

"Nineteen scholars accompanied by the head teacher, Miss Coleman, visited Crediton this after-

A percussion group. This shows Terry Jones, Pat Eastman, Roger Burley, Anne Lavercombe, Jack Cox, Michael Blackmore, Nigel Taylor, Kathleen Hind, Michael Gollop, Elvie Snow, Ian Taylor, Margaret Burley, Peter White, Maureen Holland, Margaret Johnson and Christine Shapland.

Shields and certificates won in the Devon Music Festival. Taken by Miss Coleman in 1950.

Norman Facey, Celia Budge, Delia Braunton, ?, Charles Stanbury, Pamela Rice, Diana Smart, Harold Heale, John Taylor, Colin Lethaby, Martin Sexon, Marlene Heale, ?, Christine Attwood, Susan Ensor, Andrew Bament, Jean Nutt, Colin Hutchings, Denise Webber, Angela Doughty and Mary Courtenay.

noon to compete in the Percussion Band Class of the music competition under the adjudicator, Dr Thomas Armstrong. Our band was awarded a First Class Certificate and the Cecil Trophy for the second year in succession. The set piece was Tschaikovsky's March from the Symphony Pathetique."

School Log Book March 1949.

Cynthia Snowden, née Reed, 'Miss Reed', was a student teacher at Bishops Tawton for a year in 1947 and returned as a teacher 1949. She remembers having only eight pupils in her first class. The classroom was a small 'cupboard like' room off the infant area. For those who know the school that cupboard is still there! Cynthia was the conductor for the percussion concerts, she remembers them well and mentioned how successful the percussion band became. The school had a good reputation especially for music. She recalls the journeys to play in competitions and tells of one occasion where she felt very ill on the way home. She caught chicken pox from the children.

School Swimming Pool

The swimming pool was a major project for the school. Parents, old boys from the school and older children helped in the construction of the area. Funds were also raised by parents, the finished pool cost over £630. It was opened by Mr Jeremy Thorpe, MP for North Devon. The pool measured 41 feet by 17 feet and it had a filtration unit. Everyone was so proud of the finished result and the pool was used for years to teach Bishops Tawton's children their swimming skills. It was also used in the school summer holidays when parents took it in turns to supervise the children. Later the area was cleared and after a

An aerial view showing the swimming pool at Bishops Tawton School.

Bishops Tawton children in their swimming pool: Norah Clements is the teacher here.

number of years a School Hall was built. The School Hall was another campaign and funds were raised over a period of time.

On 17 July 1964 the Headmaster declared that, "32 children had learned to swim since the swimming pool came into use 3 weeks ago."

In July 1964 Jeffery Lock remembers being a child in Bishops Tawton School at the time when the swimming pool was being constructed. He recalls being taken to the site to work in the afternoons with a wheelbarrow, a fork and a spade by Mr Clements the Headmaster. He said that parents helped build the pool in evenings and weekends.

Sue Squire remembers,

"A few years before I left it was decided to have an outdoor swimming pool. Every Wednesday afternoon on his half day my dad went round to people's houses asking if they would give money towards it. The pool was eventually constructed but it was difficult to try to learn to swim, as it was so cold even in the summer."

"Lollipop Lady"

As the traffic increased on the road the school employed school crossing lady.

Meg Runnalls remembers,

"I was the first lollipop lady in the village for the school. There was Mr Clements the Headmaster; he lived over the road in the School House. He came to see me one day and offered me the job. I used to look after the Herner kids. I live right in front of the school. The children from Herner had to wait for a bus to come from the Grammar School so I used to keep an eye on them and let them wait in my garage. I put up a dartboard for them to use."

Meg Runnalls, saw the children safely across the road.

The Canteen

The canteen is history now. It was demolished a little while ago. The children now eat their lunches in the hall where they are cooked in an adjoining kitchen area. At one time meals were bought in to school by the WVS and cooked at the Barnstaple British Restaurant.

In 1945, 39 children sat down to eat lunch that had been cooked in the canteen. Things were continually improved and updated; in 1945 a gas stove was installed instead of the oil one in the canteen for washing up water.

The new canteen was the pride of the school when it was new. It was opened in 1949 with an opening ceremony. Miss Smyth-Richards opened it in front of a crowd of dignitaries.

Some "dinner ladies" on the steps of the old canteen. Joan Holland, Maureen Scott, Mary Hutchings and Lena Knight.

Freedom

Children seem to have been much more free to roam with out adults supervising them. There was lots of freedom. Ronald Down remembers playing football in the road with a pig's bladder, when there were few traffic dangers in the 1920s. His daughter Sally Colwell recalls playing hopscotch and skipping in the Village Street and only being disturbed by the half hourly bus passing through the village in the 1950s. Many people remember as children they were out and unsupervised for the whole day.

In the past the village had its own resident policeman. Bill Babb remembers Mr Chapple, a policeman who he says was very strict. It was quite normal to get a cuff behind the ear and a telling off but he said,

"You did what the policeman said, as you knew he'd catch you next time! Being a village-based policeman at that time when the village was smaller, he must have known all the families and children personally."

Playgroup / Pre-school

There has been an active playgroup / pre-school in the village for many years. They met in the Village Hall for a long time and always had to clear the equipment at the end of each session. More recently they have moved into permanent accommodation at the base of the Methodist chapel. They have always had close links with Bishops Tawton School and they continue to work closely together.

Head Teachers

Different characters have come and gone. Each one influenced the development of the school in their own way. Their style was influenced by national trends and by the amount of money they could use to improve the school. All of them seem thoroughly committed and keen to move the school forward.

Who were they? Who do people remember?
Miss Sylvia Coleman

In the 1940s Miss Coleman was the Headteacher. There were two Miss Colemans, one was the Head of Herner and one here at Bishops Tawton. At Bishops Tawton, Cynthia Snowden remembers her being very 'go ahead'. She encouraged the growth of PE especially gymnastics. Her children won prizes for percussion band playing. The School Log Book records that when she resigned she was presented with a 'handsome' canteen of cutlery and a silver cake-basket. There was then a temporary Headteacher, Mr A.J.D. Chapman at Bishops Tawton School following her resignation.

Mr Clements

James Waldron remembered that Mr Clements had a cane but he didn't use it very often!

A section of the School Log Book tells us Mr Clements started at Bishops Tawton in 1951. Sadly he was only Headmaster for five years as he died suddenly at the age of fifty six. The newspaper article at the time tells us that he was keen on sport and during his time at Bishops Tawton the school became one of the first schools in the area to have its own swimming pool. He was married with three sons who were in their twenties at the time. He was a member of the local church and president of the Allotment Association.

Denise Webber remembers,

"The top class had a library off it, it was a very small room. More like a cupboard. Dick Clements was a very cultured gentleman and he used to love books and art. He actually started my love of art. Around the classroom were Van Goghs Vermeers and Rembrandt's Cavalier. I remember looking at them and day dreaming.

The staff with Mr Richard Clements, Christine Shapland, Ray Steele and others.

I remember being the library monitor sometimes. We had a fish tank on the side near the window and we all took it in turns to be fish monitor. We had to take the fish out into a jam jar and then clean it out and go and find fresh greenery because in those days you couldn't go to a pet shop and buy it."

Mr Jim Rowe

Mr Rowe was the Headmaster of a primary school in Bedfordshire for two years before coming to Bishops Tawton.

Miss Trish Isherwood

Mr Rowe, the Headmaster with his staff. taken around 1972. Some of the others in the photograph are Clive Robins, Christine Shapland, Gwen Short, Maureen Holland, Mary Hutchings and Hazel Griffiths.

Miss Trish Isherwood became Headteacher in 1986. She remembers, sadly, dealing with several tragic deaths early in her time at Bishops Tawton. She recalls Hannah Gillard a pupil, Sarah Westacott a

Miss Isherwood with her staff in 1992. Sue Theobald, Maggie Sandbach, Jane Leach, Maddie Harding, Christine Shapland, Fay Poggi, Fred Ovey, Miss Trish Isherwood and Hannah Huxtable.

Hamlyn and Alex Jones and Nicholas Tyrell took the lead parts in 1989. She recalls that the whole school was involved. Claire Keast's class was transformed into a medieval village and although it was wonderful, Trish says she almost lost one of the cleaners as a result! The theme was even carried into technology where they made rat traps!

Mrs Gill Gillet

Mrs Gillet was the next Headteacher. She came to Bishops Tawton in September 2001 and moved on to a bigger headship in Braunton in 2009. She started the present School Council and was responsible for the school's 'outstanding' Ofsted result.

Mrs Melanie Smallwood

Mrs Smallwood has been the Headteacher at Bishops Tawton School since 2009. There is a picture of her, the present head, and the school children at the end of this chapter. At this time the school is famous in the county for its netball, the team have recently come second out of the whole of Devon. Recently children have been working with the police using speed cameras to slow the traffic on the main road outside the school. The old canteen has been demolished and a new building, a log cabin, has been added to the grounds. This has been a major fundraising project and will be used by groups of children.

student teacher and Maggie Sandbach, a teacher. The school, parents and friends planted trees and bulbs to remember each one of them. A copse was planted in memory of Maggie Sandbach, a well loved teacher.

On a happier note she remembers the first musical performed by the school, it was *The Pied Piper of*

Mrs Gill Gillet with her class. Claire Coles, Jack Warren, Laurel Bromfield, Sepi Ballard Merrivale, Jake Salkeld, Rivka Shaw, Carmen Young, Beth Woolacott, Max Woolaway, Gerish Waldron, Harrison Mackenzie, Sue Lake, Edward Mann, Lauren Bange, Oliver Rhodes, Tom Elliot, Hope Boyle, Harmony Constant, Ben Evans, Carrie Dingle, Grace Walters, Debbie Passmore, Gareth Pike, Evie Gates, Jack Hogg, Saxon Phillips, Eleanor Leaper, Marcus Coyle, Peggy Leaver and Jo Southon.

The Football and Netball Teams

Bishops Tawton school has had matches against other schools and have shown skill and lots of enthusiasm over the years.

Above: *The team in 1972. Some faces are recognised, Christopher Rew, Graham Beer, Andrew Ward, Brian Down, Paul Shapland, Mark Saunders and Martin Hill.*

Top right: *The football team of 1995. Steven Ashford, Ben Quick, Tommy Lambert, Robert Heyward, Nathan Amery, Oliver James, Tim Bussel, Stewart Selly, Greg Sharples, Ross ? and Stephen Heyward.* PHOTOGRAPH BY TEMPEST.

Below: *The teams of 1992. Carla Seymour, Nathan Elliot, Gemma Witham, Kate Trevethen, Kay Hannam, Steven Dibble, Lisa Taylor, Matthew Squire, Jonny Sandbach, Joseph Pearson, Robert Down, Thomas Brailey, Darryl Spry, Laura Sharples, Daniel Woolacott, Lindsey Allen, Daniel Abbott and Sheena Jago.* PHOTOGRAPH BY TEMPEST.

The netball team. Leah Harvey, Lauren Howard, ?, Mrs Nadine Busby, Elizabeth Masters, Georgina Treanor, Alison Hill, Georgina Smithers, Emily Archer and Megan Johnson. PHOTOGRAPH BY TEMPEST.

A few class photos from the past

Taken around 1950 by Miss Coleman.

This is a class photograph from about 1960. Joy Spear, Anne Stanbury, Micky Nutt, Clive Pritchard, Jackie Attwood, Brenda Lock, Marian Hodge, Clive Pridam, Clive Watton, Richard Clements, Susan Crick, Sue Brown, Pat Courtenay, Graham Hutchings, Ian Budge and Ruth Rogers.

Many villagers remember this teacher, Mrs Mabbot. Some names were added at the Memories Exhibition. They are, Phillip Beer, Richard Shapland, Paul Hill, Jackie Hutchings, ? Willoughby, Marcus Bowden, Graham Rogers, Julie Bowden, Joanna Down, Andrew Ward, Timothy House, Edward Chapman and Clive Evans.

The School Log Book in 1951 records that two boxes of books have been sent by the Devon County Library. A children's library was started in the school and Mrs Mabbot was the librarian.

A class photo from 1975. Mark Elson is the teacher here. Children named are Joanna Baxter, ?, ?, Louise Draper, Emma James, ?, Debbie Draper, Helen Oram, ?,?,?,?, Lizzie Hill, ?,?, ?, Alison Mock, ?,?,?, Rachael Smith, ?, Helen Shapland, Terry Tumbridge, Alison White, ?, Maria Mcallester.

Mr Fred Ovey and Classroom Assistant Maddie Harding in 1994. Tommy Lambert, Stewart Selly, Steven Ashford, Robert Hayward, Paul Cluitt, Greg Sharples, Anya Krusjeski, Ben Quick, Josh Burrel, Tim Bussel, Nathan Amery, Liz Lean, Daniel Passmore, Steven Hayward, Kyla Manenti and Suzanne Holland.
PHOTOGRAPH BY TEMPEST.

1996. The teacher here is Mrs Hannah Huxtable. Pip Scott, Oran Manenti, Ryan Felkin, Craig Ridd, Elliot Macdonald, Natalie Wells, Oliver Passmore, Dominic Heap, Winston James, Nicola Spry, Julianne Johnson, Andrew Eve, Dominic Standen, Cherry Scott, Chloe Johnson, Sophie Bailey, Ben Lane and Ross Chapple.
PHOTOGRAPH BY TEMPEST.

Mr Russ Constant is the teacher here in 2000. William Treanor, Sophie Howard, Jack Stiling, Niki Felkin, Ben Lane, Laura Hill, Bradley Dymond, Dawn Prout, Mark Johnson, Lloyd Copp, Danielle ?, Jake Bater, Callum Ovey, Andrew Masters, Rebecca Price. Ryan Pike, Bryony Heap, Adam Peacock, Cherry Smithers, Amy Shelton, Ben Wormleighton, ?, and Sam Southern. PHOTOGRAPH BY TEMPEST.

Herner School

"Very cold today. Temperature 42 degrees. Impossible to use ink as it was frozen in the inkwells."
Herner School Log book.

18 December 1916.

A school was provided at Herner by Robert Chichester of Hall. It appears that the school was adapted from a stone-built barn in 1874. The School Board formed in 1885 and took over the school, leasing the premises. Under the Local Education Authority in 1902 the school continued in this building until 1958 when the remaining pupils transferred to Bishops Tawton School.

What was life like at Herner School?

After reading the Herner School Log Books it seems that life was hard for the children and staff on many occasions. There were often very high numbers of children absent from school. These absences give us glimpses into the life in school and in the village in the past.

The school served a very rural area and travel in poor weather and darkness was difficult as well as the considerable distance some children had to walk to get to school.

In March 1897 *"attendance was very bad owing to the awful stormy weather. No school on Wednesday morning as the weather was so rough the children could not attend."*

Floods were a frequent problem and a common cause of absence, sometimes even causing the school to close.

Above left: *The door to Herner School.*
Above right: *Does anyone remember the toilets? These photographs were taken by Steven Thomas. They will hold memories for many.*

Herner School as it looks today.

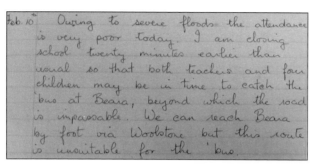

Flooding in 1950, a section of the School Log Book.

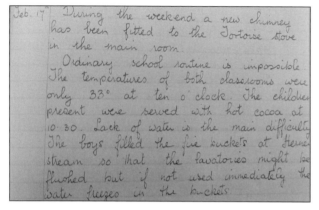

A cold winter in 1947, a section from the School Log Book.

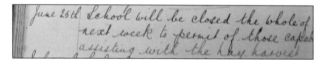

The hay harvest in 1915, from the School Log Book.

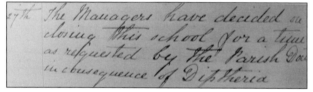

Health was a cause of many absences. Diphtheria in 1877.

In 1877 on 22 October it is recorded that a child was *"withdrawn from school on account of there being no convenience for crossing the river in winter."*

December 1919, *"Five children gone home to change their boots and stockings – got wet through carrying the little ones over the water which flooded the road."*

In 1950, *"November 21st, only 14 children out of a possible 30. The rest are cut off by the flooded conditions of the roads. Those present have reached school under great difficulties."*

There are many entries that tell us how difficult life was inside the school. Heating was an issue. The chimney smoked and frequently made the room unusable. In January 1948 it tells us that *"supplies of coke are exhausted and it was very difficult to keep the fires burning in the schoolroom."*

Children were also absent for helping on the land.

There is another entry where several children have been absent in October for picking up potatoes. More recently pupils remember having time away from school to pick the daffodils which were sent off in the train to London to be sold.

The Chichesters from Hall remained an important part of the school there are many records of Mr Charles Chichester and his wife being in school, listening to readers, teaching singing and scripture to the children.

There is a report in the *North Devon Journal* for August 1952 that tells us that Miss E. Drummond who was the Headmistress of Herner School left village life behind her and went to teach in Trinidad in the Caribbean.

This shows a group of children at Herner School in the1940's. Taken by Miss Coleman. Dora Gollop was the classroon assistant. The children have been identified as Ken Smith, Sid Smith, Ken Hutchings, Colin Shapland, Alan Huxtable, Gordon Short, Phillip Huxtable, George Shapland and Bobbie Barrow.

Bob Barrow remembers his first day at school when he was taken to school by his aunt and was knocked to the ground by a boy called Sid and rescued by a girl called Alma Wheaton who he later met at the reunion. She was in a wheel chair in 2002 and he pushed her chair in and left her with friends. She thanked him and he thanked her for rescuing him in 1939.

He also remembers the garden behind the school where they grew potatoes. He recalls sheep breaking into the garden and destroying all their work. On one occasion during wartime the children went out collecting hips and haws and they were sent to Bristol for Rosehip Syrup. He used to be late for school and was always getting reprimanded for this he would walk to school and spent time 'bird nesting' on the way.

Hugh Thomas remembers,

"I went to Herner with my sisters. I don't suppose I ever thought I would have anything to do with Hall estate when I went to Herner. There was the time when the bus got flooded at Herner corner and we had to get out and walk through this huge puddle: it wasn't very deep but it came over our shoes. We had to take our shoes and socks off at school and dry them on the boiler."

John Shapland from Queensland, Australia wrote a letter because he could not attend the reunion. He writes of many memories.

"The novelty of flushing the toilet as many children did not have that at home. The collection of rosehips to be turned into rosehip syrup."

He writes,

"The authorities decided that every child should have one third of a pint of milk each day and this was dropped off at the church corner every day by the black door. Two boys had the job each morning of collecting the crate of milk and returning to

George Shapland's report from Herner School in 1943.

school. Each side of the black door was a wall covered in ivy and our aim was to turn the ivy brown and over some months we achieved it by taking turns to piddle up over the ivy whilst the other one kept watch."

Pupils remember it as a happy time in their lives where they were very in touch with the seasons and nature.

In 2002 there was a reunion for pupils who had attended Herner School.

Bishops Tawton School in 2012. Mrs Mel Smallwood is the Headteacher. PHOTOGRAPH BY TEMPEST.

Bishops Tawton School
The Present and the Future!

Now what is the future of Bishops Tawton?
The children at school were asked to imagine the village of Bishops Tawton in the future. The following pictures and writing are thoughts and ideas from children throughout the school. Their ages vary from four to eleven years.

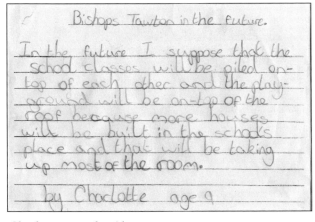

Charlotte wrote her ideas.

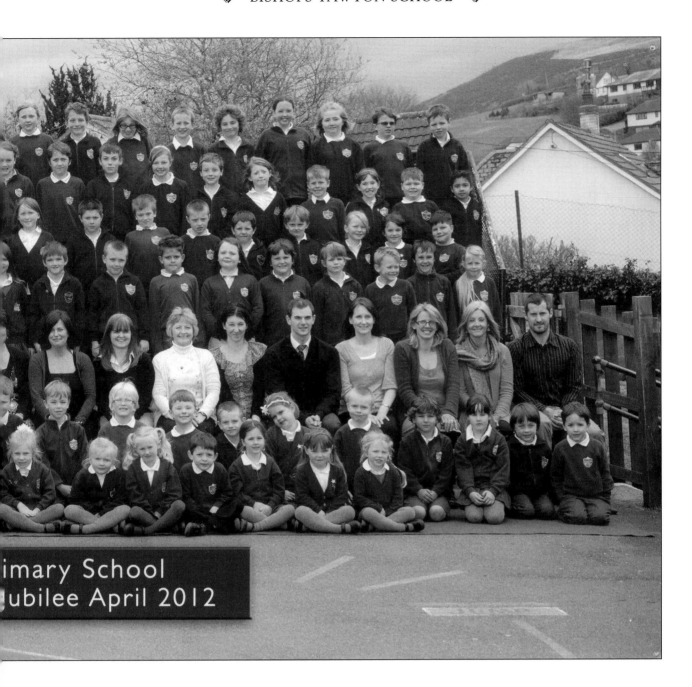

Bishops Tawton in the Future

In the future i would belive that there will be way more houses a lot bigger buildings and possibly hotels. I could imagine that there would be one big castle on Codden Hill with more visitors coming to stay. I would expect the river Taw to be much wider and bigger because there will be more water, and possibly some ships or Kaya

By Joseph Pin age 9 Years

Joseph predicts the future for the village.

Bishops Tawton in the future

In 50 years... In the future I imgine the School will be a Floating alien Space ship high in the Sky because aliens will invade our country In the Future I predict that bishops tawton will become an amazon Jungle because of the weathnt changes in bt.

by Shay age 9

This is written by Shay.

In the future...

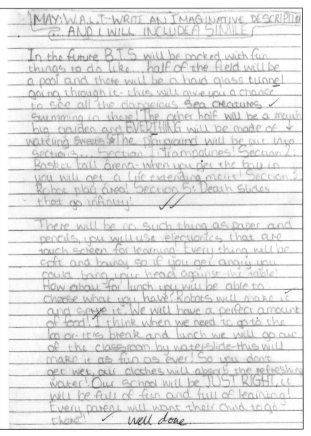

the cherch is covered in culifil metorll swetess.

colourful metal
Sweeties

Molly.

Molly thinks there will be colourful metal sweeties on the church.

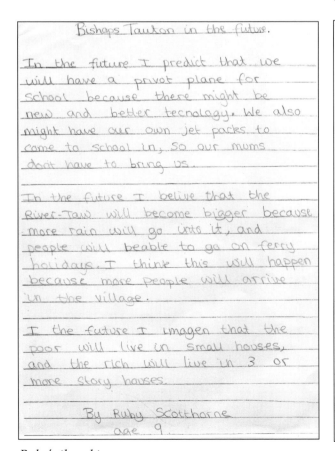

Bishops Tawton in the future.

In the future I predict that we will have a privot plane for School because there might be new and better tecnology. We also might have our own jet packs to come to school in, so our mums dont have to bring us.

In the future I belive that the River-Taw will become bigger because more rain will go into it, and people will beable to go on ferry holidays. I think this will happen because more people will arrive in the village.

I the future I imagen that the poor will live in small houses, and the rich will live in 3 or more story houses.

By Ruby Scotthorne age 9.

Ruby's thoughts.

MAY: W.A.L.T-WRITE AN IMAGINATIVE DESCRIPTION AND I WILL INCLUDE A SIMILE

In the future B.T.S will be packed with fun things to do like. half of the field will be a pool and there will be a hard glass tunnel going through it. this will give you a chance to see all the dangerous sea creatures swimming in there! The other half will be a mouth big garden and EVERTHING will be made of wateling sweets! The Playground will be put into sections... Section 1: Trampolines! Section 2: Basketball arena-when you get the ball in you will get a life extending mout! Section 3 Robot play area! Section 5: Death slides that go infinity!

There will be no such thing as paper and pencils, you will use electronics that are touch screen for learning. Every thing will be soft and bouncy so if you get angry you could bang your head against the table! How about for lunch you will be able to choose what you have? Robots will make it and serve it. We will have a perfect amount of food! I think when we need to go to the loo or it is break and lunch we will go our of the classroom by waterslide-this will make it as fun as ever! So you dont get wet, our clothes will absorb the refreshing water! Our school will be JUST RIGHT, it will be full of fun and full of learning! Every parent will want their child to go there! well done.

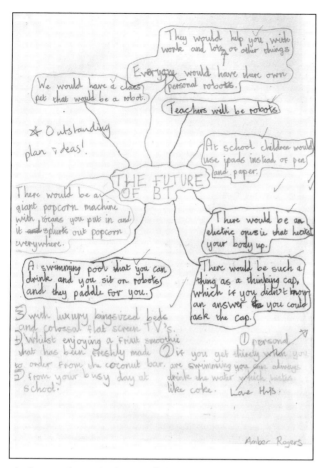

Amber made a mind map of ideas.

Ellie's ideas.

Maylee has some interesting ideas.

Subscribers

Elvie Aldridge

Nathan Amery

Miss Katrina Andrew, Well Close, Barnstaple

Mrs Patricia Andrew

Diane and Roger Andrews

Mr and Mrs Baglow, Mount Pleasant,
    Bishops Tawton

Denise Ball (née Webber), Bideford

Sue Barker

Bob Barrow, Homepark, Lovacott

John and Shirley Baxter, Old Barn, Bishops Tawton

Michael and Stella Beer, Bishops Tawton

Graham R. Beer, Linisfarne Way, Torquay

Phil and Chantelle Beer and family,
    Green Meadow Drive, Pilton, Barnstaple

Mr and Mrs Bingham, Pilton, Barnstaple,
    North Devon

Roy Blackmore, son of Bill and Ruby Blackmore,
    born and bred in Bishops Tawton

Maureen and Brian Body, Barnstaple

Peggy Bonner, Village Street

Delia Mary Braunton, 11 Park Villas

Michael William Braunton, 11 Park Villas

Laurel Bromfield, Bishops Tawton

Cherry Bromfield, Bishops Tawton

Cynthia Casey

Barbara Chaplin

Berwick Coates, Bishops Tawton, Devon

Suzy and Jamie Conchie, Whitemoor Farm,
    Bishops Tawton

M. Courtenay, Chapelton, North Devon

Ron and Sally Crook, The Bungalow, Chestwood

Lynn and Bill Dare, Easter Street, Bishops Tawton

David Down, Hayne, Bishops Tawton

Ronald Down

Ossie Down

Eddie P. Dymond, 'Venn Vale', Bishops Tawton

Mrs Mavis Eastaugh

Pauline J. Eayres, Ewhurst, Bishops Tawton,
    North Devon

Mr and Mrs Elliott, Bushens, Bishops Tawton,
    North Devon

Colin Elworthy, Bickle, Swimbridge

Margaret Evans (Langmead), David & Roy Evan,
    (Interred in churchyard)

W. and G. Facey, formerly Fairview Cottages,
    Bishops Tawton

Jean Ford

Sophie Ford, Bishops Tawton

Christina Forder-Blakeman (née Wyborn),
    Bishops Tawton

The French family, Cranford, Chestwood,
    Bishops Tawton

Ashley and Alison Fulford, Hammetts Lane,
    Bishops Tawton

Mrs W. Gayton (née Houle), formerly Springfield
    Cottages, Bishops Tawton

L.W. and S.J. Geen

Susan Gough

Miss Laura J. Gregory, Chestwood, Bishops Tawton,
    North Devon

Mr James D. Gregory, Chestwood, Bishops Tawton,
    North Devon

Ann Harris, Wellington, Somerset

Yvonne Heale, South View

Syd Hillman, 'Four Oaks', Chestwood, Bishops Tawton (1960-65)

Brian and Jill Hogg

Suzanne Holland

Christina Holland

Barry Hooper, Easter Combe Cottages

P. J. and E. Hopkins, formerly Fairview Cottages, Bishops Tawton

Joanne and Bryce Horrell, New Zealand

Mr and Mrs E. J. Houle and Mary, Lillian, Margaret, Wendy & Kenneth, formerly Springfield Cottages Bishops Tawton

S. Huxtable-Selly, Cobbaton

Rob Jenkins, brought up in village

C. Jones (née Courtenay), Chapelton, North Devon

Sally Joy (née Jenkins), Barnstaple

Miss Megan L. Knight, Chestwood, Bishops Tawton, North Devon

The Knights of Bishops Tawton

Rebecca Lange

Alison Langfield, Plymouth, Devon

Julie and Sandy Learmonth

Pete Leaver, Bishops Tawton

Anita Lethbridge (née Down), Bishops Tawton, Devon

Pamela and Clifford Lewis, Chestwood Villas, Bishops Tawton

Carl and Suzanne Lewis, Barnstaple

David and Claire Lewis, Barnstaple

Eileen M. Ley, Park Villas, Bishops Tawton

Tim Luxford, Welwyn Garden City

Chris Luxford, Plymouth

Iain Luxford, Umuarama, Brazil

Sylvia and Ernie Luxton, Bishops Tawton

Diane J. Lyddon, South View, Bishops Tawton

Mrs Laura Manning (née Sharples), previously of Sentry Lane, Bishops Tawton

Dave and Rose Mason, Mount Pleasant

Sam McKernan, Halmpstone

Sylvia Mercer

D. and D. F. Millen, Deer Wood View, Bishops Tawton

Chris and Marian Morrison, 2 Mill Cottage, Bishops Tawton

Mike and Vanessa Newey, Mount Pleasant, Bishops Tawton, North Devon

Diana and Bill Nicholls

Jean Norman (née Shapland)

Sarah Oram

Helen Oram

Terry and Christine Palfrey, Bishops Tawton

Olive Parkhouse, East Street, Bishops Tawton

Pat Parkhouse

Mr J. P. Partridge FRCS., Tawton House

P. P. and J. Pay, Valley Cottages, Bishops Tawton (flood victims)

Tom and Liz Peacock

Howard Pearson and family, Mount Pleasant, Bishops Tawton

Julie Philipps and Ross Warmington, The Old Forge B&B

Ivan Pollard, Bishops Tawton

John Rice

Sheila Ridd (formerly Hills View, Bishops Tawton)

Norman and Gwen Rider, Oatlands Avenue, Bishops Tawton, North Devon

J. Ridgeon (née Courtenay), Glastonbury, Somerset

Paul, Amanda and Alice Robinson, Hills View, The Square

Gerald Rogers

Anthony and Penelope Rogers, Bishops Tawton

Matthew Sanders, Germany

Dean Sanders, Torquay

Jean Shapland, Herner, Bishops Tawton

George and Christine Shapland

Paul Shapland

Mr Leslie Shapland, Herner, Bishops Tawton

Trish Sherwood, B.T.C.P. School, 1986-2001

Andy Shiner, Mount Pleasant, Bishops Tawton

William Slee, Sydney, Australia

Mr M. J. Snell, Taw View Terrace, Bishops Tawton

Esta Snell, Bishops Tawton

Bessie Snell, Bishops Tawton

Gillian Snow

Cynthia Snowden (née Reed), Northam

Phyllis Spear, 'Myrander', Sentry Lane, Bishops Tawton

Andrew J. Spear, Codden Farm, Bishops Tawton

Susan M. Squire, Bratton Fleming, North Devon

Andrew J. Squire, Basingstoke, Hampshire

Peggy and Toni Stacey, Nettleham, Lincoln

Charles and Jane Stanbury, Halmpstone Farm

Charles Stanbury, Halmpstone

Jayne Standen (née Shapland)

Jenny Stevens, lived all her life in the village and farmed at Whitemoor Farm

Wilf Stevens

Mary Stevens (née Beer)

Ian Stewart, Village Street, Bishops Tawton

Roger Stow

Michael Sturges, Sentry Lane, Bishops Tawton

Jane Sugars, Barnstaple

Mavis Symons (née Eayres), Phillip Avenue, Barnstaple

Ian Taylor, Bishops Tawton

Hugh Thomas, Elm House, Bishops Tawton

Richard and Dorcas Tossell

Ingrid and Richard Vain, Bishops Tawton

Karen and Bill Varney, Hastings, Sussex

Jill and James Waldron

Alan and Avril Watts

Adrian Watts (grew up in the Village)

Shaun Watts (grew up in the Village)

Tristan Watts (grew up in the Village)

Katie Wells, Fremington, Barnstaple, North Devon

Mrs Vicky Slee White, Highwinds, Barnstaple

Guy Williams, Chittlehampton

Lee Williams, Chantry Barton

Mr C. K. and Mrs L. E. Willoughby and Graham, Gary and Nicky, Park Villas, Bishops Tawton

Betty Wilson

A. and B. Woollacott, 2 Hills View, Bishops Tawton

Gary and Linda Wright, (married in Bishops Tawton church 1987)